52
WEEKS

TO
FINANCIAL
FITNESS

52 WEEKS

TO

FINANCIAL

FITNESS

The Week-by-Week Plan for
Making Your Money Grow

MARSHALL LOEB

CROWN
BUSINESS
NEW YORK

Published by Crown Business, New York, New York. Member of the
Crown Publishing Group.

Random House, Inc. New York, Toronto, London, Sydney, Auckland
www.randomhouse.com

CROWN BUSINESS and colophon are trademarks
of Random House, Inc.

Printed in the United States of America

Library of Congress Cataloging-in-Publication Data

Loeb, Marshall.
    52 weeks to financial fitness : the week-by-week plan for making
your money grow / Marshall Loeb. — 1st ed.
        p.   cm.
    1. Finance, Personal.   I. Title: Fifty-two weeks to financial fitness.
II. Title.
HG179.L5516   2001
332.024—dc21

                                                              00-064416

ISBN 0-8129-3337-0

10 9 8 7 6 5 4 3 2 1

First Edition

For Peggy, Michael, Margaret, Marjorie,
Michael II, Katie, Caroline, Jeremy, Marc . . .
and More TK

ACKNOWLEDGMENTS

Many talented and dedicated people helped me in creating this book, and I am profoundly grateful to all of them:

Frank Merrick, my longtime friend and colleague at *Money* and *Time* magazines, brought his deep knowledge and exceptional writing skills to the job of helping draft many of the chapters.

John Mahaney, an editor and a gentleman, gave me great encouragement in this work, kept me on schedule and, in all, distinctly enhanced the book.

John Castro, ably aided by editorial assistant Elizabeth Carson, did a remarkably thorough job of fact-checking the entire manuscript, running down countless sources, and never hesitating to challenge the author. He also made numerous valuable editorial suggestions.

Elyssa Folk, who has a brilliant journalistic career ahead of her, contributed to several chapters and largely wrote Week 9, Master the Computer, a subject in which she is an expert.

Maryan Malone smoothly handled the copy-editing and made many useful suggestions.

Michele Perri, efficiency expert *extraordinaire,* helped me organize and keep track of the material that went into the 52 chapters.

Warren M. Bergstein, Certified Public Accountant and professor of accounting and taxation at Long Island University, was a sure-footed guide through the maze of tax law, expertly and patiently answering our endless questions.

I'm also deeply appreciative for the major editorial contributions made by Glenn Daily on insurance; Denise Topolnicki on wills and trusts; and Emily Andren on powers of attorney.

Among the professional financial advisers and tax experts who made significant contributions were Lu Anne Morrison, Randy Siller, Stanley Altmark, Jim Weikart, and Richard Prince. The lawyers to whom I'm grateful are Alan Kroll, Gary Greenberg, and Harry Peden.

Alexandra Lebenthal, Jim Lebenthal, and Barry Bostwick illuminated the subject of tax-free bonds for me.

Other important contributions were made by Greg McBride and John Schaffer at bankrate.com; Peter Hollenbach and Sheila Nelson of Bureau of the Public Debt; Susan Stawick of the Internal Revenue Service; Mark Rosen of the Consumer Credit Counseling Service; Louise Meng, Sonia Ordenes-White, and Mary Lee Kingsley of the Bank-Fund Staff Federal Credit Union; Amy Plympton of LIMRA; Dean Maki and David Brown of the Federal Reserve Board; Professors John Langbein of Yale and Richard Wellman of the University of Georgia; Karen McKenzie of the Urban Institute; Russ Podhurst of Atlantic Business Association; Salvatore Costa of the Sterling National Bank; Keith Gumbinger of HSH Associates; and Jason Zweig of *Money* magazine.

A very personal thanks goes to Roger Donald, a book editor with a fine knack for picking winners, for his consistent confidence in this project.

Acknowledgments

Finally, the title for this book arose from an expansive dinner that Peggy Loeb, my ever-patient roommate, and I had with our children, Michael and Margaret. I don't recall which of them came up with the ultimate wording, so I credit, and thank, each and all of them—for that, and so much, *much* more.

M.L.

CONTENTS

Contents

Contents

INTRODUCTION

Look at this book as your personal trainer—your friendly, expert, immediately useful, personal trainer.

You know that the time has come to get into better shape, financially.

For most people, just getting started is the hard part. But once you're on your way, you'll wonder how you ever performed at your peak without your personal trainer.

No matter what kind of condition you're in now, your trainer will—week by week—carefully bring you to the next level.

In sum, your trainer—this book—will show you, step by step, how you can become financially fit. Every week, you will have a measurable and reasonable task that you can accomplish—or at least get a good start on.

The first week out, we'll get you to perform a little work on the treadmill. We'll do simple things like making sure that you are collecting the highest interest available on your savings and checking accounts. Then, a short time later, we'll go into a bit of weight training by having you learn to use some personal finance software. Soon after that, we'll make sure you are putting your money into the right IRA for your circumstances. Next, we'll do some heavier lifting by pursuing some profitable strategies for buying stocks and reinvesting dividends.

There's nothing extreme here—no Triathlon spurts of futures or options. You don't have to take those kinds of risks.

Getting your personal finances into good long-term shape is a demanding and often daunting job. But the work needed is much easier—and you are more likely to succeed—if you do one task at a time.

We have divided your job of effecting a financial plan into 52 pieces, one week each. We do not expect you to complete everything involved with each task in just one week. We do expect that you will get a strong start on it, while recognizing that you will have to continue pursuing each specific goal for a long while to come.

As you follow the practical suggestions in this book, you will feel better with every passing day. At the end of 52 weeks, you should have considerably greater control of your finances. And you can build from there. Staying fit will be something that you work at every day—profitably—for the rest of your life.

52 WEEKS

TO
FINANCIAL
FITNESS

Score Some Quick Wins

W ho says there are no second chances? Every dawning day gives us all a fresh start, a new opportunity to begin making all the moves needed to get our finances in shape—at last! Remember: It's seldom too late, and never too early, to start investing and saving intelligently, and to take other steps that are necessary to improve your financial health.

Let me share with you 10 of the most important steps I've learned over the years. Several may sound familiar to you; together, they create a useful checklist of sensible moves toward financial security. Consider them as a few quick hits—ways to make or save money *immediately*. All of them—and much more—will be detailed in the pages of this book. Start taking one or more of these steps this week, then follow up with others in subsequent weeks.

Step 1

Visit your bank and find out how much interest you're collecting on your checking, savings, and other accounts. Ask a bank officer how you can collect a somewhat higher rate of interest. Many banks and savings institutions pay their bigger savers more; you may be able to get an extra point or so tacked onto your savings—just for asking. After all, you're a good customer, and the bank wants to keep your business. Perhaps you can switch your cash from an ordinary savings account to a higher-yielding bank money market account or even a short-term certificate of deposit (CD). If you have $5,000 or more to put into a CD, ask your banker whether that will qualify you for a special bonus rate.

Step 2

Before your next payday, arrange with your bank—or your employer—to have a fixed amount deducted from every paycheck and deposited into your savings or investment account. Often, a bank will automatically transfer money—$25 or more each month—from your checking account to a stock mutual fund of your choice. Usually, there's no fee for this service.

Step 3

Put up to $5,000 a year—in *pretax* dollars—into a Flexible Spending Account (FSA) for dependent care, if your employer offers such a plan. (Most do.) In effect, the dollars you put into FSAs are *not* taxed. Use the tax-free FSA funds to pay for the care of your dependent children or a disabled spouse or relative. You can also employ FSAs to pay for health care for you and your family—and save a ton on taxes.

Step 4

Start a tax-saving Individual Retirement Account (IRA). You and your spouse can contribute up to $2,000 each a year, and all the earnings on that money—dividends, interest, and capital gains—will be tax-free until you withdraw it. You also can deduct that $2,000 a year from your taxable income, so long as: (1) You are not covered by a pension plan already, or (2) Your adjusted gross income is less than $52,000 if you're married or $32,000 if you're single. (Married people who earn less than $62,000 and singles who earn less than $42,000 get a partial deduction.) It's remarkable how fast your contributions can grow. Say that you were lucky enough—and smart enough!—to have started at age 21 to put $2,000 a year into an IRA. If you earn and reinvest an average of 9 percent on the money, you'll have more than $1 million by the time you're 65.

Step 5

You may choose to take advantage of the new, improved version: the Roth IRA. You can withdraw all your contributions to a Roth and your earnings on them, totally *tax-free,* provided you meet certain conditions. You must:

> Have held the IRA for five years; and
> a. Reached 59½ years of age; or
> b. Have passed away (the funds will be disbursed to your heirs); or
> c. Have become disabled; or
> d. Use the funds to pay for Qualified First Time Home Buyer expenses.

With a traditional IRA, you have to pay ordinary income tax on your money when you take it out.

Step 6

Check that you have one of these in place: a 401(k) plan; or a 403(b) plan if you work at a school or other nonprofit organization; or a 457 plan, if your job is in a state or local government agency. For each dollar you contribute, many employers add 50 cents or more to your account. That's found money. If you already have a 401(k), review how much you're putting into it, and consider whether you should kick in more. Of the income you earned in 2000, you can contribute up to $10,500 to a 401(k) or 403(b) plan. Here's a potential bonus: Because the money you invest in a 401(k) is not considered part of your adjusted gross income, your contribution *lowers* your adjusted gross income (AGI), perhaps making it possible for you to deduct your IRA contributions from your taxable income.

Step 7

Be sure you are not overwithholding taxes from your paycheck. Many people do that just to build up a rich cash refund from the IRS. Bad idea! You're giving an interest-free loan to Uncle Sam. Tell your employer's payroll department to increase the number of your dependents. You'll get an automatic pay raise, and you can use the found money to buy into a stock mutual fund or a money fund.

Step 8

Resolve to take every tax-saving step that you reasonably and legally can. Start right now to keep detailed records of your contributions to charity and any deductible expenses that are necessary for doing your job, such as your gasoline and parking fees when you drive to clients and make sales calls.

Step 9

Pay off all your credit-card bills—even if you have to take out a bank loan to do so. It costs you much less to pay the loan interest than to pay the interest rate on your credit-card bills, which often hits a walloping 18 percent. Just think: If you're in the 28 percent tax bracket, you'd have to earn 25 percent on your money, before taxes, to equal what you would save by paying off your balance on a credit card that's charging you 18 percent interest.

Step 10

Start now to give money away on a regular basis to your children, your grandchildren (if you have any yet), your nieces and nephews, and other heirs. This may save them tremendous sums in federal and state estate taxes when you eventually meet your Maker. Open a custodial account for each child at a bank or brokerage house. Much or all of the income from the account—dividends, interest, and capital gains—will be taxed at your child's favorable rates. True, if the child builds up a large amount of money in his or her own name, he or she eventually may be eligible for less college aid. Even so, I've found that, for most families, it makes sense to open custodial accounts for the children.

There's much more. Read on.

Boost Your Savings: Here Are Ten Ways

You probably learned the virtues of saving at your mother's knee. Putting money aside regularly and religiously is the only way you can accumulate an emergency fund, as well as the cash you'll need for the down payment on a first house, a college education for your kids, and a comfortable retirement for you and your spouse. Systematic saving can provide you with the means to save still more money—for example, by enabling you to pay cash for your next car rather than financing the purchase.

Yet, even though thrift is thought to be a traditional American virtue, most of us don't practice it. In the first half of 2000, we set aside only 0.2 percent of our disposable income—far below the peak of 10.9 percent in 1982. That's dramatically less than the savings rate in Germany, Japan, and other industrialized nations. Of course, cultural comparisons are tricky—not to mention that each country's way of calculating savings is different—but, indisputably, Americans are lousy savers.

How much should you save? The right answer for you depends on your age and your family circumstances. But here's a plan that states the bare minimum:

- If you're 40 or younger, aim to save or invest at least 5 percent of your pretax pay.
- From age 41 to 45, step up your savings by one percentage point a year.
- After age 45, put away 10 percent a year—and preferably 15 percent.

The earlier you begin saving, the better. Consider the following facts.

Starting at age 25, if you put $2,000 a year in a money market mutual fund, which paid interest averaging about 4.84 percent in August 2000, you'll have $245,618 at age 65.

But if you don't begin saving that annual $2,000 until age 35, your savings at age 65 will total only $137,541.

In short, by getting an early start, you can almost double your savings by retirement age, thanks to the magic of compounding—that is, you earn interest on the interest you've accumulated in previous years. (For simplicity's sake, we have left the impact of taxes out of the calculations. But we're not being entirely theoretical. You could accumulate those amounts, tax-deferred, in an Individual Retirement Account or some other qualified retirement savings plan.)

Some people are able to save money with no specific purpose in mind. But most of us need one or more savings goals.

The first goal can be to accumulate an emergency fund—cash you can tap in case of illness, job loss, or some other financial disaster. Keep this money in a bank savings account, a bank money market account, or a money market fund, so that you can get at it quickly. The total should equal at least three months' living expenses. Better yet, put away six months' worth. And, if you're self-employed or your job isn't secure, sequester enough money to pay your living expenses for a full year.

After you've topped off your emergency fund, begin saving for specific short-, medium-, and long-term goals. Your short-term goals might include taking a terrific summer vacation or being able to buy certain Christmas presents. Medium-term objectives (those that are three to five years away) might be to make the down payment on a first house, or to purchase a second home or a new car. Long-term objectives for most people are simply stated: college for their children and a stress-free retirement for themselves.

How fast will your money accumulate? Here's a rule: Divide 72 by the return you expect on your savings. The answer will be how soon your money will double (before taxes, of course). Thus, if you put your savings in a money market fund paying 6 percent, your money will double in 12 years (72 divided by 6 equals 12).

Think you can't afford to save? Think again. Here are ten ways you can save money right now:

1. Cut your auto insurance premium more than 10 percent by raising your collision deductible from $250 to $500. Consider increasing it to $1,000 if you can afford to pay that much out of your own pocket for a fender-bender.

2. Ask for low-cost generic versions of expensive brand-name drugs—provided your doctor or pharmacist agrees this is advisable.

3. Save on stock market commissions by using an Internet broker, unless you need a full-service broker's research and advice. Similarly, favor no-load or low-load mutual funds over their costlier kin.

4. Use a home-equity loan (average interest rate in late September 2000: 10.25 percent) to pay off your consumer loans, particularly your credit-card balances (average interest rate: 17.36 percent). An extra bonus: Interest on the first $100,000 of home-equity loans is tax-deductible, whereas interest on credit-card debt and other consumer loans is not.

5. Refinance your old high-rate mortgage with one of today's somewhat lower-cost loans. (In late September 2000, rates on 30-year mortgages averaged about 7.92 percent.) Earmark the difference in monthly payments for savings.

6. Favor a 30-year mortgage over a 15-year one. Your monthly interest payments will be lower, and you can save the difference.

7. When you get your next raise, save it—and continue to live on your old income.

8. Channel any bonuses into savings rather than splurging on a vacation trip or a new car that you don't really need.

9. Sock away any minor windfalls, such as gifts, tax refunds, investment profits, or freelance fees.

10. Keep budgeting for debts that you've paid off. The only difference: Add the money to your savings.

Put Your Savings and Investments on Auto Pilot

Here are six painless (well, *almost* painless) plans that automatically steer part of your earnings into savings, so you won't get your hands on the money and be tempted to spend it.

You can put any of these plans into practice by filling out a simple form—provided by your employer or your bank or some other financial institution—that lets you set aside $25 a month or more. We've grouped the plans in two categories: (A) those sponsored by employers and (B) those offered by financial institutions.

Category A: Employer Plans

If your company offers an automatic deduction-and-deposit plan, grab it. Three programs are commonly available.

1. *Retirement savings plans.* Deposit money into your company's profit-sharing or stock-purchase plan if your employer offers them. Your own contributions are not tax-deferred. But taxes are postponed on (a) any money put into your account by your employer, (b) any earnings on those contributions, and (c) any earnings on your own deposits.

Similarly, take advantage of any other retirement savings plan your employer offers—for example, 401(k) at private companies, 403(b) at schools and other nonprofit organizations, and 457 at state and local government agencies. Of the income you earned in 2000, you can contribute up to $10,500, tax-deferred, to a 401(k) or 403(b). Many employers contribute 50 cents or so for each dollar you put into your plan, up to a maximum of 6 percent of your pay.

2. *U.S. Savings Bond plans.* Figure out how much money you want withheld from your pay—from $1 per paycheck to $25,000 a year—and your employer will invest the money for you in Series EE Savings Bonds. Ask your payroll department for the enrollment form. Interest on your bonds is exempt from state and local taxes, and you pay no federal tax on the interest until you cash in the bonds when they mature. (The time it takes to collect the face amount on an EE bond depends on current interest rates. In mid-2000, when the EE bond rate was 5.73 percent, EE bonds would mature in 12 years.)

Better yet, if your adjusted gross income is below a certain total, you can avoid some or all of the federal tax on your EE or I bond interest *if* you use the proceeds to pay college or vocational-school tuition for yourself, your spouse, or your children. The income ceilings for full deductions in 2000 were $79,650 for married couples filing jointly and $53,100 for single persons. You could get partial deductions for income between $79,651 and $109,650 for married couples and between $53,101 and $68,100 for single persons. The ceilings rise with inflation, so check with the federal government before adopting this strategy. (For the latest bond yields and income limits, call the Bureau of Public Debt at 1-800-487-2663 or visit its website at www.publicdebt.treas.gov.)

3. *Deferred compensation plans.* Many companies offer these plans to highly paid employees who can afford to postpone taking some of their income until they need the money—say, at retirement. You only need to tell your payroll department to defer a bonus, or some of your salary, until an agreed-on time.

The advantage: You're not taxed on the money until you receive it. Perhaps you will then be in a lower tax bracket than you are now.

The disadvantage: Tax law doesn't permit your employer to guarantee that it will pay you the money. (If the company did, you would owe taxes on the deferred income, since you would technically be in receipt of it.) This leaves your money vulnerable to being seized by creditors if the company runs into financial trouble.

The obvious advice: If your employer looks shaky, don't sign up for a deferred-compensation plan.

Category B: Private Plans

1. *Dividend-reinvestment plans (DRIPs).* These plans allow you to plow your dividends into additional shares without paying commissions—and, sometimes, at slightly lower prices. At last count, nearly 1,000 publicly traded companies offered DRIPs. Some plans charge small fees, but they're still far lower than the commissions you would pay to a full-service broker. (For more on DRIPs, see Week 29: Make Your Money Grow—Drop by Drop.)

2. *Transfers from a checking to a savings account.* As a bank depositor, you can often arrange to have a fixed sum of money switched from your checking to your savings account or to a higher-paying money market account. You set the amount—typically, the range is from $25 a month to as much as you wish. You can get the authorization form at your bank.

   Warning: Don't forget to allow for the automatic transfer in your personal budgeting or you'll risk overdrawing your checking account.

3. *Transfers from a bank account to a mutual fund.* Stock and bond funds often accept transfers (typically, $25 a month or more) from checking accounts. Usually, there's no fee for the service. You can withdraw the money whenever you wish—for example, when you need to buy a new car. Ask the fund of your choice for an application form, or ask your stockbroker, if you opened your mutual fund account through him or her. When you send back the completed application, attach a blank personal check. (Don't forget to write "VOID" on the face of the check!) You can cancel the arrangement at any time by calling the fund or your broker.

All these plans have one principle in common: Pay yourself first. Whether you follow this strategy with an automatic savings plan or on your own, it's the best way to pile up assets fast, so that you can handle most of your financial problems and ensure lifelong financial security for yourself and your family.

Contribute the Max to Your Employer's Savings and Investment Plans

This is the week to check that you are making the most of the retirement savings plans sponsored by your employer. They have various names. For-profit companies sponsor the famous 401(k) accounts; nonprofits such as schools, churches, and charities offer 403(b) plans; state and local governments maintain 457 plans. (The numbers indicate the federal tax code sections that permit the plans.) Small firms offer SIMPLE accounts, or Savings Incentive Match Plans for Employees.

No matter what your plan is called, the questions you face are the same: Are you putting as much as you should into your account? Are you investing your money too conservatively?

Your plan is most likely a dynamite deal. With Social Security's future uncertain and with the decline of traditional pensions—the kind that require no contributions from employees—you are increasingly responsible for your own security in retirement. The best way to pile up the assets you'll need is with an employer-sponsored savings plan that provides for *tax-deferred compound growth*.

You elect to put part of each paycheck into the plan. Your contribution isn't considered immediate income, so it's not taxed immediately. You can invest your contributions in stocks, bonds, and other assets, and the earnings on them will compound tax-free until you take them out of the account—usually not until you retire. When you do retire, your withdrawals will be taxed at regular income tax rates.

Employer-sponsored savings plans are often terrific benefits, for two reasons:

1. Most companies match a portion of their employees' contributions. This match generally ranges from 25 cents to $1.00 for every dollar the worker puts in, up to a certain dollar limit or a percentage limit—typically, $2,000 or 3 percent to 6 percent of earnings. Let's say your employer matches your contributions dollar-for-dollar up to $2,000. If you put that much into your account, you'll automatically double your money. Invest $6,000, and your company's match of $2,000 will equal a 33 percent annual return—roughly equal to the stock market's glorious performance in the late 1990s!

2. Taxes are postponed on your investment earnings and contributions—up to the maximums described below—until you start withdrawing money from the account, usually after you retire. This enables your

nest egg to grow much faster than if it were regularly raided by taxes.

Let's say you invest $6,000 a year (after taxes) at an 8 percent annual return and you're in the 40 percent tax bracket. In 20 years, your *taxable* account would total about $274,572. But what if you put the money into a 401(k), 403(b), or other *tax-deferred* account? Your contribution will come from pretax earnings, so your annual investment can amount to $10,500, at no more out-of-pocket cost to you than in our first example. Over 20 years, an 8 percent annual return will turn your investments into $457,620—roughly 66 percent more than in a taxable account.

You don't have to lose the benefits of tax-deferred compounding if you change jobs. If your balance totals more than $5,000, your original employer must allow you to leave your money in the plan if you wish.

But most benefits departments will encourage you to take the money. If you do, don't ask for a check. If you accept a check, assuming you're under age 59½, you'll most likely owe a 10 percent tax penalty plus regular federal and state income tax on your money—a whack that could amount to as much as 60 percent of your balance! Instead, enroll in your new employer's retirement savings plan as soon as that employer allows you to. Then ask the new plan's administrator to arrange for a transfer of your old account's balance into your new one. You won't have access to the money, so you'll owe no tax on it.

Alternatively, you can roll the money over into an Individual Retirement Account (IRA). Just be sure to have your former employer transfer the money *directly to your IRA*. If the company makes out the check to you, it will have to withhold 20 percent of your balance to cover potential taxes. You would then have to come up with the missing 20 percent elsewhere and deposit the entire amount into your IRA within 60 days to avoid taxes and perhaps a 10 percent penalty. (The federal government would refund the withheld 20 percent after you file your tax return.)

How much should you put into your account? For a detailed answer, you can use the worksheets in Week 46: Calculate What You Will Need in Retirement. Or, you can turn for help to a financial planner or to computer software such as Quicken Deluxe 2000, priced between $45.00 and $60.00.

Federal law limits contributions to company-sponsored plans. Of the money you earned in 2000, you could kick in $10,500 to a 401(k) or 403(b) plan, or $6,000 to a SIMPLE plan. The ceilings will rise with inflation.

Many plans allow you to make additional contributions from your *after-tax* earnings. But your combined employee and employer contributions can't exceed 25 percent of your pretax pay. If you're a "highly compensated employee," meaning you earn more than $80,000 or own more than 5 percent of the capital in the business, you may face still further limits.

Most Americans invest too little in their tax-deferred savings plans, but there's also a danger in investing too much in these plans. After all, you probably have some other pressing goals—for example, buying a home or sending your kids to college. You can take money from a tax-deferred account before retirement, but unless you're 59½ or older, the withdrawal will generally be socked with a 10 percent penalty in addition to regular income taxes. (The penalty is waived if you withdraw money early to pay for medical expenses that amount to more than 7.5 percent of your adjusted gross income. Also, the penalty does not apply to early distributions from 457 plans.)

Most employers let you borrow against your 401(k). Tax law allows you to borrow up to $50,000 or 50 percent of the amount that is vested—whichever is less. The interest rate is likely to be lower than the rate you would pay to a bank or other commercial lender. You repay the loan with payroll deductions that can be spread over five years—or longer, if you're buying a home. Also, your interest payments go into your account, so, in effect, you're repaying yourself for the loan. Meanwhile, all of your money not on loan keeps earning tax-sheltered income.

On the other hand, unless the interest you're paying yourself is a higher rate than you are earning on your investments in the tax-deferred account, borrowing from it may not be wise. The chief reason is that you'll miss out on the tax-deferred compounding you would gain on the money if you hadn't borrowed it. Also, these loans usually must be paid if you leave your job. If you can't come up with the money, the loan balance will be treated as taxable income. You then may have to pay the 10 percent penalty, on top of the regular income tax on the outstanding loan.

One overall conclusion is: When you decide how much you should tuck away in your tax-deferred account, be sure not to lose sight of your other financial goals.

Another key consideration: Are you investing your money too cautiously? Unlike traditional pension plans, a 401(k) or other tax-deferred savings plan does not promise you a specific pension amount at retirement. Instead, your benefit will hinge on your contributions and your investment returns. Depending on the plan, you may be offered as few as three investment choices or, more commonly, 10 to 12, including small-company and large-company U.S. stock mutual funds, an international stock fund, U.S. bond and money market funds, guaranteed investment contracts (GICs), and your employer's stock. If your plan does not give you enough choice, complain to your benefits department.

Many people put too much money in low-yielding investments like money market funds and GICs, and too little in stocks. Sure, stocks are riskier, but history's lesson is that, over the long run, they offer far greater growth potential than fixed-income investments. Indeed, if you are in your twenties, your thirties, or even your forties, there is a strong argument that you would do well to put just about all your 401(k) money into stocks or stock mutual funds. If that strategy sounds too chancy, remember that you may already have one low-risk nest egg in Social Security and perhaps a second in your company's pension plan.

As you get closer to retirement, you should take fewer risks by gradually moving your portfolio into more conservative investments: Treasury securities, blue-chip stocks, high-dividend stocks, and growth-and-income and income mutual funds. When you're 10 years from retirement, financial experts suggest that your investment portfolio—including both taxable and tax-deferred accounts—might look like this:

- 35 percent large-company stocks (or stock funds).
- 20 percent small-company stocks.
- 15 percent international stocks.

- 20 percent high-quality bonds.
- 10 percent high-yield bonds.

(For more on asset allocation, see Week 25: Choose the Right Investment Mix.)

Yes, you can have both a company-sponsored savings plan and an IRA. You might want to have both, even if you cannot deduct your IRA contributions from your taxable income. (For the rules, see Week 43: Open an IRA—or a Roth IRA.) But if you must choose one over the other, you might be better off with a 401(k). First, the annual contribution limits are higher with a tax-deferred company plan than with an IRA—up to $10,500 versus $2,000. Second, if your company offers a match—even a miserly 25 cents on every dollar you put up—the 401(k), 403(b), or other employer-sponsored plan probably wins hands down.

Alternative Plans

If you have a choice of several company-sponsored savings plans, park your cash in the one that offers the highest company match. Besides 401(k) accounts, companies sometimes offer:

- *Profit-sharing programs.* The employer makes annual cash deposits into employees' accounts. The amount may depend on the size of each year's corporate earnings, but it doesn't have to. Employees may also be able to add deposits of their own.

- *Stock purchase programs.* In this plan, you might have the choice of contributing 3 to 6 percent of your pre-tax salary. Often, a company will ante up $1 for every $2 you contribute. All that money goes to buy the company's own stock. Warning: Beware of investing so heavily in your employer's stock that most of your assets wind up in that one issue. A reverse in the firm's fortunes could leave you with nest egg on your face. A tip: Try to keep your holdings in your company's stock from exceeding 10 percent of your assets.

Open a Flexible Spending Account

Health care expenses are devouring more and more of our family budgets, and many medical bills strike when we least expect them. Still, there are some costs not fully covered by health insurance that you can foresee—maintenance drugs and orthodontia, for example—and it's wise to build a reserve of money to address these bills. One sound way to do that, and beat the rising costs of health care, is to enroll in a Flexible Spending Account (FSA) where you work.

If your employer offers you an FSA, you'd probably be smart to contribute to it.

Most of the Fortune 500 companies—and many others as well—have FSAs. Particularly in these times when it is hard to find and retain reliable workers, companies like to see their employees healthy and happy.

Workers embrace the FSAs: millions of Americans have such accounts. Their popularity also is symptomatic of the trend toward letting workers personalize their compensation packages, choosing between pay and benefits and selecting specific kinds of benefits.

With an FSA, you can set aside part of your *pretax* earnings to pay for health care for yourself and your whole family. You also can use it for dependent care for your kids and aged relatives. The FSA money is not taxed, so you save a bundle on taxes. In brief, the IRS enables employers to offer their workers a choice between taxable cash and a variety of *nontaxable* benefits.

To pay for those benefits, you can set aside part of your salary, up to certain annual limits set by your employer or the IRS. The ceilings may rise as high as $5,000 for health care and another $5,000 for dependent care (although you can choose to contribute much less). A number of employers even contribute 50 cents or a dollar for every dollar that you put in. You then can use this tax-free money to pay for a wide range of services—generally, those not fully covered by health insurance. They may include health insurance premiums; medical, dental, and vision deductibles and co-payments; prescription drug, mental health, and substance abuse treatment co-payments; certain smoking cessation programs; eyeglasses and laser eye surgery; tutoring for certain learning disabilities; special equipment installed in your home or car for medical reasons; and, in some cases, acupuncture or the services of a Christian Science practitioner.

In the dependent care area, you can use your nontaxable FSA dollars to pay for baby sitters, nursery schools, child care centers and day camps, or expenses for elder care centers or for a housekeeper to look after an aged parent or some other relative who is dependent on you.

Of course, there are a number of medical services that FSAs will *not* pay for. They include marriage counseling fees, maternity clothes, health clubs, weight reduction programs, hair replacement treatments, and cosmetic surgery.

For more information about eligible expenses, call 1-800-TAX-FORM and ask for IRS publication 502 (for medical and dental expenses) or 503 (for child and dependent care expenses). You can also retrieve publications online, at www.irs.gov. One warning: You *must* spend all your FSA money in the year you set it aside. In short, use it or lose it.

Figure Out What You Are Really Worth

Not long ago, the Gallup Organization discovered that Americans' most popular New Year's resolution was no longer losing weight or quitting smoking, which had topped the list for the previous 12 years. Instead, today's Americans most want to manage their personal finances better. And no wonder: After nine fat years of rising prosperity, more and more people are discovering that, no matter how much they earn, smart financial planning offers the surest way of reaching their goals. Perhaps you want to buy your first house, or to send your kids to college, or to become financially independent and retire early. Whatever your goal, reaching it starts with the two tasks scheduled for this week and Week 7:

1. Learn what you are worth today.
2. Make a budget you can keep, so that you will be worth more tomorrow.

Calculate Your Net Worth

Before you tally actual figures, jot down your best guess at your net worth. Later, you are likely to discover that you are worth a lot more than you thought.

Using some pencils, some record sheets, and a calculator—or a computer software package such as Quicken or Microsoft Money—write down the current value of all your possessions. They might include:

- Your checking and savings accounts and your money market fund.
- Any stocks, bonds, mutual fund shares, and other securities.
- The value of your investments in any tax-deferred retirement plans, such as 401(k)s, 403(b)s, IRAs, and so on.
- The current cash value of your life insurance policy (not counting term coverage, which has no cash value). If your annual policy contract update doesn't state the amount, ask your agent for it.
- Your employee benefits, which might include profit-sharing and retirement savings accounts, unexercised stock options, and the lump-sum value of an employer-paid pension, if you're covered by one at work. (Your employee benefits department can tell you the current amount.)
- The estimated market price of your house or condo, if you're a homeowner. Ask a real estate agent for a quick appraisal, or note the asking prices of similar homes for sale in your neighborhood.

- The estimated market price of any second home, vacation condo, or time share that you may own.
- The resale prices of art, antiques, jewelry, or other collectibles you own. If you need to call in an appraiser, expect to pay him or her $100 to $300 an hour.
- The resale value of your automobile(s) and other vehicles. Either ask a dealer for estimates or consult reference works, such as the quarterly *Edmund's Used Car Prices,* at your library.
- A rough guess at the market value of your furniture, clothing, bicycles, and other personal property. (Be realistic; you couldn't sell them for much.)

    Add up the value of your possessions. The total represents your assets.

Your next step is to calculate what you owe by totaling the following:

- The mortgages, home-equity loans, or lines of credit on your real estate.
- The outstanding balances on your credit and charge cards.
- The unpaid portions of your auto loans.
- The remaining balances on your student loans.
- Any other debts, such as unsecured bank loans, margin loans with your broker, insurance-policy loans, and amounts borrowed from family members.
- The estimated capital gains or income taxes you will someday have to pay on your investment profits.

The total of these debts comprises your liabilities.

Subtract your liabilities from your assets to arrive at your net worth. If the amount is a negative figure, turn immediately to Week 18: Control Your Debt. Most likely, however, your net worth will be a positive figure, giving you a firm foundation on which to build a winning financial plan.

Recalculate your net worth at least once a year. Some debt counselors urge clients to take this financial snapshot just before they start Christmas shopping—the time of year when even the most frugal person is tempted to break his or her budget.

Find Out Where Your Money Goes

Next, figure out how you and your family are spending your money. You can't draw up a useful budget until you know how much cash is coming in every year and how much is going out—and for what purposes. Once you know all that, you can take control of your finances and set yourself on the proper course to reaching your goals.

In calculating what professionals call a cash-flow statement, figure out your income and expenditures for a calendar year. If you use a full 12 months, you help ensure that your calculations won't be thrown off by seasonal expenses, such as a summer vacation. And you won't understate expenses that occur only quarterly or annually, such as insurance bills, property taxes, and investments in IRAs.

To prepare your cash-flow statement, list all of your annual income: your salary or wages; earnings from self-employment; interest or dividends from investments; any alimony or child-support payments you receive; pension, Social Security, unemployment, or disability payments; rents and royalties; trust fund and annuity payments; and cash gifts. To make sure you don't overlook anything, review the income you reported on last year's federal tax return.

Next, list all your expenses for the year. This is harder than calculating your income because nearly everyone loses track of small expenditures, especially those made with cash. But, for your purposes, a useful cash-flow statement doesn't require accounting for every penny.

Begin drawing up your cash-flow statement by gathering together all records of expenses you can find: your checkbook, your credit-card records, last year's tax return, and any receipts you saved from cash purchases. Many of these expenses will be recorded on a daily, weekly, or monthly basis, so you'll have to convert them to annual figures, just as you did with your income.

Next, list your expenses, starting with the big annual *fixed* costs: federal, state, and local income taxes; Social Security and Medicare taxes; real estate and other property taxes; rent or mortgage payments; installment loan payments; utility payments, including telephone bills; the cost of maintaining, repairing, and improving your home; the cost of repairing and maintaining your automobile(s); insurance payments; child-care, tuition, and camp expenses; savings and investments, including any sums automatically deducted from your bank account or paycheck—for example, for retirement savings plans.

Next, add up your *variable* expenses—the amounts you spend for food at home and in restaurants; clothing and shoes; everyday household expenses; furniture and other household equipment; transportation expenses, including gas and oil for your auto(s) and commuting costs; out-of-pocket medical and dental expenses; fees for services from professionals (lawyers, accountants, or financial planners); hobby and entertainment expenses; pet-care costs; gifts to family members, friends, and charities; work-related expenses such as uniforms or union dues; vacation costs; alimony or child-support payments; miscellaneous expenses, ranging from haircuts and perfume to books, magazines, and newspapers.

Then, subtract your yearly expenses from your yearly income. Unless you're unusually diligent about keeping records, you'll find a sizable gap between your recorded expenses and your income. Indeed, when Frank Merrick, a financial journalist in Summit, New Jersey, and his wife Susan drew up their cash-flow statement, they couldn't account for about 20 percent of their spending!

To close the gap, you'll have to do what they did: Keep a written diary of every cash expenditure for a month—better yet, for two months—to avoid having any unusual expense, such as an impulse buy at a flea market, from drastically throwing off your accounting. Next, multiply the two-month total of your cash expenses by six, to arrive at an annual figure.

Don't worry if your income and outgo figures still are off by a few percentage points. That's common, and only an obsessive bean counter would want to close the gap completely. After all, you're looking for a *rough approximation* that can give you a clearer idea of where your money is going. When you know that, you will be ready to prepare a budget for spending your money more wisely and boosting your saving and investing.

Design a Realistic
Family Budget

Creating a budget that really works requires input from your whole family: You are all in this together. Begin your budget making this week by having a family council meeting with your spouse (if you're married) and your teenage children (if you have any).

Hand paper and a pencil to everyone. Agree that each of you should state, in writing, your personal financial goals. (Your children should jot down the goals they want to reach before they become self-supporting.) Be as precise as possible. Don't just note that you want to buy a new auto in five years; describe the make, and check car ads or call a dealer to learn the price.

After you've recorded all your key goals, divide them into three categories: (1) short-term (those you want to reach within the next year); (2) medium-term (those you want to hit within a decade or so); and (3) long-term (those you hope to accomplish by the time you reach retirement age).

To help stimulate your thinking, here are some typical goals of middle-income Americans, depending on their life stages:

- *Short-term.* Build an emergency fund; buy a modest car or a first home; prepare for having a child; send children to summer camp or private school; take a summer vacation; buy life insurance; make ends meet; reduce debt.
- *Medium-term.* Trade up to a bigger house; remodel or improve the present home; buy a vacation house; send children to college; take courses or earn a new degree to improve earning power; plan for a career change; buy a new car or make another big purchase, such as new furniture or a boat; take a trip overseas; achieve a more luxurious lifestyle.
- *Long-range.* Take an unpaid leave from work; start a business; plan for children's weddings; help children meet goals such as buying a first home; retire early; live comfortably in retirement.

Now, set priorities on your goals, using numbers (1, 2, 3, and so on). Think in terms of what's important, what isn't, and when you want to reach your goals. For instance, if you've been running up awesome credit-card balances, you'd be wise to make paying them down your number-one short-term goal. Your top long-term goal probably will be establishing a comfortable life in retirement.

Compare your lists with those of your other family members. You'll find some agreement—you all probably set a high priority on college education for the kids—but you most likely also will have disagreements. You may have been hoping that your children would go to relatively inexpensive public colleges, but they want to attend costlier private schools. Few families can meet each member's expectations, so you'll have to compromise.

Now write down all the goals to which everybody assigned a high priority. Talk over the ones on which you disagree, and cross off any that you all readily agree are unrealistic—say, that chateau you've always dreamed of buying in the French wine country, or that ranch in glorious Montana.

Most families won't be able to reach total agreement. But, with lists in hand, you'll find it easier to reach compromises and arrive at a final list of affordable goals.

Remember to keep your family's financial goals up to date. Review them—and your progress toward meeting them—at least once a year. If you can cross off any goals that you've met, your self-confidence will get a powerful lift. Add new goals as your circumstances change. You might also reset your goals every time there's a major change in your life—a new baby, a marriage or divorce, a new job, a move, or the purchase of a new home.

With your goals defined, you're ready to design a *real* budget—not the pretend one you've been keeping in your head for years. As your starting point, use the cash-flow statement you drew up in Week 6. It showed you how your family is currently spending its money. The budget you're about to write will state how much you think you should be spending in each category of your cash-flow statement. This will enable you to reduce any overspending and free up money for saving and investing.

You'll probably need only three months to gain control over your income and outgo. The payoff can be extremely gratifying: Investing just a few hundred dollars more every month can make a tremendous difference in your net worth over time. At a readily achievable 8 percent annual rate of growth, your money will double in nine years, triple in 15 years, quadruple in 19 years, and quintuple in 21 years. The message: You simply can't afford *not* to fight—and *win*—the battle of the budget.

Here's your next strategy. Again have a family sit-down. Refer to all the categories of spending you listed in your cash-flow statement, but now separate them into two types:

1. *Fixed expenses* that range from hard to impossible to reduce, such as insurance premiums, rent and mortgage payments, property tax bills, utility bills, school tuition, and the like. One purpose of this analysis is to help you plan for irregular but necessary and inevitable expenses, so that you will never again have to invade your savings or investments to pay them. Another purpose is to inspire you to search for ways to trim even the expenses that you regard as uncuttable. For example, by following the advice in later chapters of this book, you might find many ways to reduce your taxes, improve your insurance coverage for less than you're paying now, or take advantage of lower interest rates by refinancing your mortgage.

2. *Discretionary expenses* that you could easily reduce even if you don't want to. They include everything

from child-care expenses and clothing purchases to vacations and restaurant meals. Also include credit-card repayments; if you're carrying big balances, your top priority should be to eliminate them.

Calculate what percentage of your income flows to each expense category. Then, go through your discretionary expenses item by item, figuring out how you can trim excesses. Don't be too tight *or* too loose. If your budget is excessively strict, you may fall off the wagon. Your aim in the first of the three months is to prepare a budget that you can keep. Here are some benchmarks you might find useful:

- Allocate no more than 65 percent of your take-home pay for regular monthly expenses, including food, utilities, and rent or mortgage payments.
- Allow another 20 percent for occasional outlays, such as for clothes, household repairs, and recreation. (Don't go nuts and try to eliminate all luxuries. If you are passionate about movies and want to see three or four a week, reel back in some other area.)
- Put aside 10 percent for necessary expenses that hit at different but predictable intervals, such as insurance premiums and property taxes.
- Devote the last 5 percent—or more, if possible—to savings and investments. Don't rest with just 5 percent. Most professional advisers will urge you to save or invest 10 percent or more. But aiming that high at the outset could be a turnoff. You might not be able to stay on target, no matter how hard you try. Best advice: Start with 5 percent and then increase your

savings by one percentage point every three months or so, until you achieve the maximum that your income and lifestyle can sustain.

If you find that 5 percent is too high a hurdle, you're probably living beyond your means. The time has come to consider moving to a less expensive house, driving a cheaper car, or taking other drastic action. Otherwise, you risk running into serious trouble. You can't possibly achieve the goals that you and your family have set for yourselves unless you reduce your spending.

During the second month, try to stick scrupulously to the spending targets in your budget. (To help you keep sound records—and rein in impulse spending—you might pay for all items over $25 with checks, and let your checkbook serve as your expense ledger.) Don't worry if you overspend or underspend in a few categories by a couple of dollars; too much attention to detail will drive any sane person off his or her budget. Be sure, however, not to spend more than your after-tax income.

At the end of the second month, adjust your budget only where it is absolutely necessary. You may have set too low a spending limit on essentials like at-home food and transportation, or too high a limit on restaurant meals, tickets to sports events, or other costly fun and games.

After the third month, confer again with your spouse and older children and create a detailed review of how you've all been doing. Go through your budget's discretionary spending item-by-item once again, looking for new ways to save. Repeat your review at the end of every following year, to make sure you're staying on course. If you are, there isn't a compelling reason to rewrite your spending plan.

If you find fresh economies during any of your reviews, you might reward yourself with an extra luxury or, better yet, two. You'll have earned them.

Set Up a Sensible Filing System for Your Records

My wife, God bless her, is always urging me to clean out our old financial records—all those ancient checks and receipts that take up half the garage already. But I'm a compulsive collector. I believe that you should save just about everything, just about forever. So, how long should you *really* hang on to your documents?

Smart financial planning depends on careful record keeping, but that doesn't mean you have to save every unguided missive that lands in your mailbox. You have to be a disciplined paper trailer, knowing which documents you can safely toss and which you have to preserve for a year or more—or, in some instances, for the rest of your life.

Too much of a chore? Then consider these scenarios: An IRS auditor questions a large tax deduction, but you've thrown away the receipts. The possible result: extra tax, interest, and penalties. Or, you lose all your personal belongings in a fire, and you don't have receipts, appraisals, and photos to prove to your insurance company what you owned and what it was worth. The possible result: You'll get a smaller settlement than you deserve, and if you take a tax deduction for the unreimbursed loss—you guessed it—you may get an audit at which you'll have no way to produce the evidence you need to head off additional taxes, interest, and penalties.

This is the week to set up a system that will keep such unpleasant surprises from happening to you.

The basic rule of record keeping is: Save for at least three years anything involving your income tax. The IRS can order an audit up to three years after you file. But, this can stretch to six years if the IRS believes you underreported your income by 25 percent or more, and to *forever* if the auditors think you committed fraud.

Bottom line: If you're not a neatnik, hold for six years all your 1099s, W2s, and other tax forms, plus all records that support your deductions.

Keep some records permanently. Store in a safe-deposit box your basic real estate records. Retain the receipts for projects that qualify as capital improvements—anything that adds to the value of your home, from a built-in barbecue to a new bathroom. They may well reduce the taxes on your profits when you sell your house.

Records of contributions, distributions, and rollovers for IRAs or other retirement plans probably should be kept forever.

Records generally fall into two categories: (1) those you can keep in a cabinet at home, and (2) those that are so important you must store them in a safe-deposit box at your bank or trust company (or keep them in a fireproof safe at home, if you want them close at hand).

Let's start with the documents you must keep absolutely safe:

- *Real estate records,* including the deed to your home, documents relating to its purchase, your mortgage contract, and receipts for capital improvements. You may need all of these documents to minimize any taxable capital gain when you sell the house. If you own a second home, save the same records for it— again, for tax purposes when you sell it.

- *Receipts for valuables.* Jewelry, furs, antiques, and the like should be covered by riders attached to your homeowner's insurance policy, as explained in Week 34: Protect Your Possessions with Homeowners' Insurance. Unless you bought the items recently and have receipts, get them appraised by professionals. Store the appraisals in your safe-deposit box, along with photos or a video of the items. If your valuables are lost, stolen, or destroyed, you'll need both written evidence—and in some cases photographic evidence—to be sure of collecting what you're owed from your insurance company.

- *Investment documents.* Store certificates of ownership for stocks, bonds, or other securities in your safe-deposit box, if you don't leave them with your broker. You can keep brokerage statements and records of dividend and interest payments at home.

- *Other important documents.* Keep a list of your insurance policies and your agents' names and phone numbers in your safe-deposit box; you may store the policies themselves at home. Your safe-deposit box also is the best place for the titles to your cars, your birth and marriage certificates, your children's birth certificates or adoption papers, and other vital documents that would be difficult or time-consuming to replace. Warning: Don't keep your power of attorney, living will, or will in your safe-deposit box. Many states make it difficult for heirs or family members to open the box. Instead, leave these documents with your lawyer.

There are basically four types of documents you can store at home: the records you need to (1) ride herd on the family budget; (2) manage your investments; (3) head off trouble with the IRS; and (4) provide proof of any loss to your insurance company. Let's take them in order.

1. *Budget-related documents.* Here we include all the records of routine income and outgo in the course of daily living: pay stubs, credit-card statements, copies of bills and canceled checks—everything you need to make sure your spending is on track. If necessary, the checks can also serve as proof that you've paid a bill. Similarly, if a credit-card account is charged twice for the same purchase, the statements will prove that a mistake was made.

Keep these records in a large accordion file or a handful of manila folders, and label each expense category. You can toss out records of minor daily purchases after a year. But be careful to preserve receipts and canceled checks for valuable items; you'll need both to prove their worth to your insurance company in case of theft or calamities covered by your homeowner's policy.

Retain all warranty statements covering your major appliances or electronic equipment, along with the sales receipts and canceled checks, until you replace the appliances or equipment. Finally, save records for your nonmortgage loans; when you've paid off the debts, you have to keep only the statements that say so.

2. *Investment records.* As mentioned, keep stock certificates and other securities ownership certificates in your safe-deposit box. But, in your accordion file or manila folders, save monthly statements from your brokerage firm or mutual fund companies. You can throw them out when you receive your annual statements (after making sure that the annual date include all your transactions for the past 12 months). Save your annual statements indefinitely. Two exceptions to this rule: Hang on to your trade confirmation and dividend-reinvestment statements indefinitely; you'll need them to figure your gains (or losses) for tax purposes after/if you sell the investments. Similarly, preserve all yearly statements from tax-deferred retirement accounts, such as IRAs, 401(k)s, 403(b)s, and other employer-sponsored plans (or Keoghs and SEPs, if you're self-employed).

3. *Tax records.* To save lots of time if you do your own tax return—or lots of money if you hire someone to do it for you—follow this simple rule: Preserve everything that could conceivably save you tax money or headaches, either now or in the future. A list of vital documents you must hang onto includes the W-2 and 1099 forms that you receive after January 1, annual brokerage and mutual fund statements, records of retirement-plan payments and withdrawals, medical bills, and health-plan reimbursement statements.

The list may go on and on, depending on your circumstances. Other possible items include: receipts for real estate taxes, charitable donations, job-hunting expenses and relocation costs, and child-care services; the Social Security numbers of your children and of nannies and other household employees; year-end paychecks showing cumulative deductions for health insurance, retirement plans, and charitable contributions; casualty and theft records.

If you are divorced, keep records of alimony and child-care payments made or received, your ex-spouse's Social Security number, and a copy of the divorce decree.

Other tax-related documents that you should keep are: statements of interest on mortgages and home-equity loans; K-1 tax forms and other financial records for limited partnerships, S corporations, estates, and trusts. Keep a log of unreimbursed business expenses, such as mileage driven in your own car, receipts for car rentals, and fares for public transportation, including taxis.

In sum, save all canceled checks for business expenses, charitable donations, and any other expense that might be deductible.

After you have filed your annual tax return, stuff all the supporting documents and records in a large envelope and label it to identify the tax year. (For more on the documents you must keep for tax purposes, get IRS Publication No. 552, *Record Keeping for Individuals;* phone 1-800-TAX-FORM or visit the IRS on the World Wide Web at www.irs.gov.)

Now, for a bit of relief in your record keeping. Unless you need a document for tax purposes or if you're certain it can be easily replaced, you don't need to save it. Here's a list of records you might considering throwing away:

- *Monthly brokerage and mutual fund statements,* after you receive your annual statements and have double-checked to make sure they record all your transactions.
- *Old investment transaction and dividend-reinvestment records,* but not until six years after you sell the asset.
- *Out-of-date investment information,* including old annual reports, proxies, and promotional brochures.
- *Expired insurance policies,* as well as policies that you've allowed to lapse.
- *Old wills, powers of attorney, and living wills or health-care proxies* for which you now have new documents that are properly dated, signed, and witnessed. Don't keep the old versions. They may simply lead to confusion.
- *Pay stubs* after you receive your annual W-2 from your employer and have double-checked its accuracy.
- *Receipts and canceled checks* that are a year old (or older), unless you need them for tax reasons; in that case, hold them for six full years.

Use common sense in weeding out your files. If you're having a dispute with a merchant over a credit-card charge, for example, don't throw out the documentation until you've settled the matter.

Master the Computer

Anyone not using a personal computer to help manage his or her finances is wasting one of the best wealth-building tools ever put into the hands of the public.

Many people are still intimidated by financial software; they believe that it is too complicated to use and that the Internet is too vast to benefit from. After all, they wonder, what other inanimate object is capable of getting a virus? And if you are among those who think "URL" stands for United Republic of Liberia or that "Yahoo!" is for cowboys, you may profit from a crash course in computer science. You'll be amazed at how the Internet and financial planning software can help you whip your finances in order, save a ton of cash, and conduct deep research into investment opportunities.

Here's a primer on using your PC as your chief aid for money management.

Getting Started

As computers are finding their way into just about every American home, they're becoming increasingly affordable. A complete package typically costs $1,000 (though you can spend much more) and is likely to include: a 56-kilobyte (56K or 56KB) modem to connect to the Internet, a 17-inch monitor, a digital video disk (DVD) player for movies and CDs, a scanner to copy text and images onto your computer, and an inkjet printer for turning what you see on your screen into hard copy.

After you set up your computer, you'll need an Internet Service Provider (ISP in computerspeak) to supply the software and service necessary to use the Internet. America Online (AOL) charges a monthly fee of up to $21.95 and has huge appeal, largely because it is user-friendly. Other ISPs offer Internet service at slightly lower prices. Among them are Earthlink and AT&T Worldnet, at roughly $20 a month. Some, such as NetZero and Bluelight.com, give you services free.

Check your mail for special offers, too. Chances are that ISPs are sending you literature or actual software and may offer to connect you to the Net for a modest monthly charge, or for free. But a warning to computer novices: Free Internet services generally do not provide technical support, so if your Internet service goes belly-up at 2:00 A.M., you'll be thankful for AOL's free 24-hour assistance hotline.

The Internet offers a multitude of websites devoted to personal finance. Many other sites publish news stories about IPOs, stock splits, paying for college, planning for retirement, and similar topics.

Quicken.com and Moneycentral.com are financial planning sites that provide free personalized information and advice on investing, retirement, mortgages, wills, taxes, saving and spending, and paying for college. You can use these sites to estimate your tax liability, calculate your anticipated future income, and find the best mortgage and insurance rates. Bill payment services are also available on these two sites; they charge a few dollars per month, and quicken.com even has a limited service for free. With online bill paying, you give the website permission to notify your bank to withdraw money from your account and send it electronically, or on paper, to make regular auto, mortgage, or other loan payments.

Yahoo! (www.yahoo.com), an Internet portal, is known for its Web directory, which functions like a telephone book for websites. If you punch a keyword or phrase such as "Roth IRA" or "retirement" into its search engine—a tool that finds websites via listings of keywords or phrases—a list of all the related sites in its directory will pop up on your screen.

To compare rates and apply for a mortgage, Quicken loans at www.Quickenloans.quicken.com is a valuable resource. You can receive personalized quotes for mortgage loans, check to see whether your bid has been approved, and read articles about home buying—all online.

Bankrate.com lists current interest rates on various kinds of mortgages, auto loans, other personal loans, and savings deposits. The site compares those figures to the rates a week ago and six months ago, and has financial calculators—such as "compare the cost of living between cities" and "which credit card is best for you"—to assist your decision making.

Insweb.com and Quotesmith.com are clearinghouses for all types of insurance, from renters' policies to pet coverage. You can compare rates, read the insurance policies, and, in many cases, apply online.

Remember, once you have Internet service, you can get all this information—and much more—free. If you have specific needs—for example, if you are considering converting your traditional IRA to a Roth but don't know whether the shift makes financial sense—searching the Web can turn up Roth conversion calculators and helpful phone numbers of brokerage firms.

Many people pay fees to a living, breathing financial planner who advises them on bookkeeping, investing, tax strategy, insurance needs, planning for retirement, and paying for college. For about $60, you can get much of the same counsel from programs like Intuit's Quicken (www.intuit .com) and Microsoft's Money (www.microsoft.com).

Microsoft and Intuit are the titans of personal finance software. In their battle for computer users' business, they are always rolling out new user-friendly products. Installation is a breeze; expect to spend about 10 minutes on either Money or Quicken. After you install the program, you are guided step-by-step to write in your personal information: income, investment assets, retirement accounts, and expenses. Quicken sells about three times as many programs as Money, but computer experts say it's a close call in determining which is better.

Here are some features that both Money and Quicken offer:

- Spreadsheets, worksheets, and calculators to chart expenses and categorize them in areas such as education, home, auto, and entertainment.
- A service, working in conjunction with your bank, that pays bills online and transfers money between your accounts.
- A portfolio tracker with real-time quotes and news updates from the Web on stocks, bonds, mutual funds, and other investments that you own or wish to follow.
- Tax help to estimate your liability and figure out which expenses are deductible; also, tax law updates and tax-cutting tips.
- Retirement income/spending advice, preparation of a will, and estate-planning advice and spreadsheets.
- Budget planners, including a debt-reduction tool that (1) prioritizes paying off high-interest debts, and (2) projects when you'll be out of debt.

Microsoft Money has several distinguishing features. Its homepage lets you decide, when you begin each Money session, what information is to appear on your screen. You choose from Web articles of interest, bill reminders, an investment summary, and more. After you install Money and fill out your personal information, the program will recommend the features that will be most useful to you.

Quicken is known for its easy data entry and large number of planning tools. Entering your personal information can be time-consuming and tedious, but Quicken eases this burden with a transaction register that transfers your information to its correct place in the program. Or, if you have been using Quicken.com and then buy the Quicken software, you can transfer all of your data to the program within seconds.

Additionally, "What If?" scenarios let you determine the impact of increased income or depreciated investments, among many other variants, on your finances. Quicken's deduction finder is very sharp; it recognizes words like *babysitting* and *child care* as deductible expenses of the same kind. You can also bookmark the tools of the software that you use often.

Tax programs can help you prepare your income tax returns faster and more accurately than by hand, and they may uncover more deductions than you otherwise would. Intuit's TurboTax and Kiplinger's TaxCut are industry leaders in tax-preparation software. These programs ask you to answer questions about your income and expenses. The information you give is placed in its proper spot on your tax return, and you then have the option to print it and mail it in, or file it electronically.

By enabling you to calculate your tax liability, these programs save you the grief of trying to make sense of IRS forms. Based on the information that you provide, every legal deduction that you qualify for will be taken. The programs are relatively inexpensive; prices start at $29.95 for TurboTax and $14.95 for TaxCut.

You can also download TaxAct from Second Story Software. It is similar to TurboTax and TaxCut, but it is available free of charge. Visit www.taxact.com for more information on how to get TaxAct.

Several websites deserve mention for cutting-edge technology. Here are three that are popular with visitors:

1. Paytrust.com and Paymybills.com are two sites that can move your bills from one desktop to another: from the desk you sit at, to your PC. Sign up with one of these services and your bills will be sent straight to the Internet company's office where they will be scanned. An image of them will then appear online. You will receive an E-mail each time a new bill arrives. You can authorize payment from your savings, checking, or bank money market account. The service costs about $9 a month for up to 25 transactions. (Keep in mind that you probably spend just under $200 a year on postage and on printed checks.)

2. Yodlee.com and www.verticalone.com have created the technology to unite sites that are often used for financial matters. Each consumer's account information is protected under one screen name and one password. Normally, when you enter personal information into a website—for example, a retirement planning site or a tax advice site—you will be prompted for a screen name and password. If you use many websites for your personal finances, you must remember many names and codes. But Yodlee and VerticalOne have partnered with a large number of financial sites and, together, they protect your personal data under one name and password. The hitch is that your favorite sites may not be included on their list of partners.

3. E*trade.com and Fidelity.com are just two of the many sites that let you trade stocks, options, bonds, mutual funds, and commodities online. That means

no more waiting for your broker to call you back. These sites vary in the commissions they charge. Some provide thorough market analysis and long-term advice. Others offer fast order execution and charge low commissions. But this warning has come from personal finance columnist Terry Savage: "That immediacy of response can also be a tremendous temptation to get in over your head." For more on brokerages, both traditional and online, see Week 26: Find the Best Broker for You.

Find—and Get the Most from—a Tax Pro

Filling out any year's tax forms is only part of the job. Ask yourself whether you would benefit from hiring an adviser who will meet with you as often as necessary to help you plan and carry out a strategy for cutting your taxes *year after year.*

You probably don't require such professional help if your tax situation is relatively uncomplicated. You should be able to fill out your forms yourself with the help of a do-it-yourself tax preparation computer program such as TurboTax or MacInTax from Intuit (see www.intuit.com), or a book such as *J.K. Lasser's Your Income Tax* (Macmillan, $14.95).

Or, you can have your return prepared by H&R Block. It charges set fees, depending on the complexity of a client's tax situation, but the average charge is well under $100. You won't get any tax planning advice; however, if your finances are straightforward, you probably don't need much. Be aware that if the Internal Revenue Service raises any questions about your return, you'll have to defend it yourself or hire a knowledgeable representative. Storefront preparers aren't permitted to represent you. Again, when your tax situation is simple, you run little chance of trouble with the IRS.

If your finances are more complex—say, in the past year, you sold a house or unloaded lots of stocks or mutual fund shares—you may need a pro's help to fill out your forms properly and make sure you take all the write-offs that you're entitled to.

You can hire either a certified public accountant (CPA) or an enrolled agent. Either of these professionals can handle a complicated tax return, give you year-round tax advice, and represent you if the IRS challenges your return.

CPAs and enrolled agents undergo rigorous training. A CPA must pass a state accountancy exam to earn certification and attend continuing education classes to stay up-to-date. An enrolled agent has either worked at the IRS and earned a special license, or has passed a demanding two-day IRS test. CPAs and enrolled agents may charge $100 or more an hour or flat fees of $200 to $1,000, depending on the area you live in and the complexity of your return.

There are roughly 400,000 CPAs in the fifty states— more than ten times the number of enrolled agents—so we'll assume that you'll be hiring a CPA. (You probably should not even consider hiring a tax lawyer, unless you face a truly complex situation—for example, you and your former spouse were divorced partway through the tax year, or you are starting a business and need considerable tax advice.)

You find a tax professional much the same way as you locate any other financial adviser (see Week 27: Begin Your

Search for the Right Financial Planner). Ask for recommendations from friends, business associates, your lawyer, or a financial planner. If you want someone who will provide year-round help, you probably should launch your search no later than June or July, because the best pros' calendars are quickly filled. Also, you will be allowing yourself six months to put your planner's tax-cutting recommendations into effect. If you want someone only to do your tax return, you can wait until January.

Look for a CPA who handles tax returns for clients whose financial situation is similar to yours. If you are self-employed, for example, you want someone who is well versed in the sections of the tax law that apply to people who work for themselves. Interview at least three candidates, and try to find one whose temperament is similar to yours. For example, if you want to claim as many write-offs as you can—aggressively interpreting the tax code's many gray areas in your favor—make sure your pro is willing to take that approach. If you want to avoid a tax audit at all costs, you want a pro who shares your caution.

Ask each candidate: Who will actually do the work on your return? At many firms, low-level accountants, called "grinders," fill out tax returns. The forms are then reviewed by the CPAs, known as "finders," who sign the returns. This isn't necessarily wrong, but don't be surprised to discover that the CPA you searched for so carefully isn't the person who is preparing your return. Beware of firms that operate on a pool arrangement (your tax forms float among a number of accountants, each of whom handles a few lines). Also, watch out for CPAs who demand a percentage of your tax refund as payment. Especially steer clear of preparers who guarantee you a refund or promise to pay you an amount equal to your refund right away, and, in return, will take your endorsed IRS check. That arrangement is illegal.

During your initial interview with the CPA, listen to his or her questions. If he or she neglects to ask about the basics of your tax situation—whether you own a home, have a pension plan, or contribute to an Individual Retirement Account—you have drawn a dud. Move on to your next candidate.

When you've found the pro who suits you best, plan on meeting with him or her at least twice a year (three times if you're an active investor, own a business, or have an unexpected windfall—say, an extra-large bonus). Meet first in the late spring, perhaps after your CPA returns from his or her post-tax-season vacation. Before the meeting, the accountant should have reviewed your past two or three tax returns and any other records that he or she has requested. For example, your pro may have asked for an estimate of your income for the year, copies of your federal and state withholding forms, an estimate of your deductible expenses, the latest statements of your investment accounts, and copies of your quarterly estimated tax payments.

At a library or in a bookstore, spend some time scanning a current tax-preparation manual. Pay particular attention to sections that apply to your situation. Draw up a list of questions to ask your tax preparer; they may help him or her come up with tax-cutting ideas that suit your circumstances. At the meeting, discuss any strategies you can put into effect to cut the current year's and future years' tax bills.

A meeting in late fall is necessary only if something has happened to your finances that warrants looking for new last-minute ways to trim your taxes—for instance, your boss tells you that you've done such a superior job that you'll soon be receiving a special five- or six-figure bonus. (If that ever happens to you, your best approach, depending on your taxable income for the year, might be to ask him or her to postpone paying the bonus to you until early in the next calendar year, thus delaying the date when you have to pay the higher taxes.)

Before you and your pro decide that this meeting isn't necessary, be sure that you have kept him or her up-to-date on your financial and family situations. Don't neglect to inform him or her if you have married, bought a house, had a child, changed jobs, or done anything else that might affect your taxes. Indeed, you would be wise to get into the habit of phoning your accountant before making any important financial decision, such as whether to buy a house, transfer money to a child's name for college expenses, and so on.

Early in the new year, when you meet with your pro to discuss your tax return, arrive fully prepared with complete and up-to-date records. Accountants often complain that clients deliver boxes or bags of records and ask them to sort out the mess. This is a waste of your tax preparer's time and of your money (most accountants charge by the hour). To save time and money, keep detailed financial records, following the advice in Week 8: Set Up a Sensible Filing System for Your Records. Then, at tax time, you can quickly assemble all the records your pro will need. If your CPA sends you a detailed questionnaire to ensure you don't leave anything out, all the better. Unless you provide everything he or she needs, you could miss out on deductions and other breaks to which you are entitled.

When you get your tax return from your pro, don't sign it until you have carefully read each line and checked the figures against your records. If you don't understand how he or she arrived at a figure, ask for an explanation. After all, if the IRS finds an error, *you* will have to pay any back taxes, interest, and penalties—not the CPA who prepared your return.

Consider Fifteen Ways to Cut This Year's Taxes

Most people treat taxes—which consume roughly 40 percent of the average American household's income—as
an inevitable and irresistible force, a troublesome necessity
over which they have no control. That's far from true. You
can have considerable influence over the shape and size of
your taxes *if you act now.* After December 31, it will be too
late to do much about your taxes on this year's income, so
don't make the serious mistake of waiting until the end of
the calendar year before taking steps to reduce your bill. For
maximum savings, treat taxes as a year round issue. Assess
their impact on almost every financial move you make—borrowing, spending, or investing.

Even if you decide to join the 50 percent-plus taxpayers
who hire a professional to fill out their tax forms, you are
still chiefly responsible for taking steps to cut your taxes.
The reason: Once the year has ended, there's very little that
even the most skilled tax pro can do to save you money. So,

get ready to act now. Here are 15 moves that may ease this year's bite:

1. Contribute as much as you can to a tax-deferred retirement plan, such as a 401(k), 403(b), Individual Retirement Account, Keogh plan, or Simplified Employee Pension (SEP). All offer generally superb ways to build savings for the future—and, at the same time, reduce your current tax bill.

If you meet the rules explained in Week 43: Open an IRA—or a Roth IRA, you and a working spouse can put a total of $4,000 a year into your accounts—and trim $1,125 from your tax bill, assuming you are in the 28 percent federal tax bracket. You'll save even more if your bracket is higher.

2. Make *next* year's charitable contributions late *this* year. You have until December 31 to mail your checks to your alma mater or your favorite charities and write off the gifts on this year's tax return, even though the checks won't be cashed until after January 1. Or, make your contributions via a credit card, and pay the bill in January. For maximum savings, give highly appreciated securities to charities and take a deduction for their market value. Warning: The law limits your deduction for charitable contributions generally to 50 percent of your taxable income, so don't go overboard. (You can, however, deduct any excess on next year's tax return.)

3. Give highly appreciated investments to kids. Instead of making cash gifts to your young children or grandchildren, give them securities on which you have big paper profits. When the kids sell the securities, they'll pay tax on the gains at *their* rate, presumably 15 percent—five percentage points less than the 20 percent long-term capital gains tax you would have to pay if you are in the 28 percent bracket or above. You can reap similar tax savings by transferring highly appreciated property to low-income parents or grand-parents who are in the 15 percent bracket. (For more, see Week 13: Cut Your Taxes by Giving Money to Your Kids.)

4. Take capital losses by December 31. In early December, total the capital gains you have earned on securities you have sold during the year. (Remember: Profits on property held for a year or more are taxed by the feds as long-term capital gains, at a maximum 20 percent. Gains on property owned for less than a year are taxed at your regular maximum: up to 39.6 percent.) Scour your portfolio for losers that you can sell to offset your gains. You can subtract losses from your gains, dollar-for-dollar. If your losses exceed your gains, you can use the excess to offset up to $3,000 of regular income. Any unused losses can be carried forward to cut the following year's taxes. *Warning:* Don't let the possibility of tax savings cloud your judgment as an investor and cause you to make the mistake of selling losers that show signs of turning profitable in the near future.

5. Sell your most expensive securities first. Instruct your broker or mutual fund representative to unload the shares that cost you the *most,* not the least. That will reduce your taxable gain. Otherwise, the IRS will require you to figure your profit by the costliest method: first in, first out (FIFO).

6. Bunch your miscellaneous expenses. Those that qualify for the miscellaneous expense deduction include: union or professional dues, tax preparation and investment advisory fees, legal and accounting fees, job uniforms and tools, job-related educational expenses, and the cost of business publications—including this book. Unfortunately, you can write off such expenses only to the extent that they exceed 2 percent of your adjusted gross income. Thus, if you're close to that threshold, it may make sense to pay next year's expenses—for example, subscriptions to business and professional publications—by December 31 of this year. They will then qualify for the deduction. Alternatively, if you can't take the deduction this year but think you may be able to do so next year, you might postpone as many miscellaneous expenses as possible until after January 1.

7. Accelerate your payment of medical expenses. You're allowed to deduct medical expenses that exceed 7.5 percent of your adjusted gross income. Thus, if you incurred such heavy medical bills that you come close to that threshold, it makes sense to take one of two steps to enable you to qualify for the deduction:

a. Reduce your taxable income—for example, invest in a CD that does not pay interest until it matures next year. Don't invest in something that pays interest this year.

b. Have elective surgery or dental work done this year rather than next, to lift your medical bills above the 7.5 percent minimum.

8. Move some of next year's tax deductions into this year. During December, you might pay next year's professional dues, as well as any real estate taxes or state income taxes due in the first three or four months of the new year. If you make estimated tax payments to your state, send in the January 15 payment before year-end so that it can be deducted on this year's return.

9. Postpone taking income until next year. This strategy is easiest for small-business owners and the self-employed,

who can delay billing customers (or patients) until the very end of December so that the money will not arrive until the following year.

10. Buy six-month Treasury bills by July or later. Even though you will receive your interest when you buy the bill, you don't need to list the income on your federal tax return until the year in which the T-bill matures.

11. Don't report your kids' income on your return. The law lets you do this for any child under 14, and, in some cases, it can help reduce your taxes. But it can be a costly convenience:

a. Your child's income may be enough to lift your adjusted gross income to levels at which your deductions and exemptions will begin to be phased out.

b. The extra income may cause you to lose deductions for miscellaneous expenses, casualty losses, and medical expenses. You can write off only the amount that exceeds certain percentages of your adjusted gross income.

c. You may wind up paying more income tax to your state if it is one of the 36 (plus the District of Columbia) that peg their residents' state tax liability to their federal tax liability.

d. You'll lose the benefit of your child's standard deduction, if he or she has earned income from a job and qualifies for his or her own standard deduction.

12. Write off points if you refinance your mortgage. Points usually must be deducted over the life of a mortgage. But if you refinance the loan on your principal residence, you typically can deduct all the points on your previous mortgage that you haven't written off in previous years.

13. Check on whether you and your spouse should file separate state tax returns. Normally, spouses file joint federal *and* state returns. But 11 states let married couples file separately if they will save money by doing so.

14. Don't overlook the student-loan interest deduction. Since 1998, qualified taxpayers have been able to deduct, each year, at least $1,000 of the interest they pay on student loans. The deduction can be taken only during the first 60 months in which interest is paid. You qualify for the full deduction if your adjusted gross income, subject to some modifications, is below $60,000 for married couples filing jointly, or $40,000 for singles. The maximum deduction rises to $2,000 for income earned in 2000 and $2,500 in 2001 and thereafter.

15. Finally, this piece of advice: Don't automatically rush to make prepayments—or generate last-minute deductions in some other way—if doing so requires you to take money out of an interest-bearing account. Compare the interest you would earn by holding onto that money longer with the benefit of the tax deduction. It's usually (but not always) better to take the deduction.

Look into a Dozen More Tax-Saving Steps

Invoking the indisputable theory of that well-worn philosopher, Mae West, that too much of a great thing is wonderful, we herewith present you with still more ways to defuse those unlovely taxes.

This week, before you determine which steps you might take, spend some quality time calculating your marginal tax bracket—the top rate that is extracted from you by your friendly federal, state, and local authorities. Let's say you're married and filing jointly. After subtracting your deductions, every dollar the two of you earn over $43,050 is subject to— and diminished by—the 28 percent federal tax rate. If your income tops $104,050, every additional dollar is taxed at 31 percent. You tumble into the 36 percent bracket when your income exceeds $158,550 and income over $283,150 puts you in the top 39.6 percent bracket.

We're not done yet: In most states, you must also pay state income tax. New York City and a few other metro areas collect local income tax as well.

To calculate your top bracket, get the tax rate schedule used by the federal government and, if applicable, the schedules used by your state and locality. (You'll find them in the instructions that accompanied the tax forms sent to you in the past year.) Your top bracket is the total of the highest rate you pay on your income, after deductions, to each taxing authority. For example, if your top federal tax rate is 31 percent and your top state tax rate is 9 percent, your combined marginal rate is 40 percent. That means every dollar you invest in a tax-deferred plan this year—say, in a 401(k) retirement account—will save you 40 cents in taxes. Put another way, the dollar that you invest via your 401(k) costs you only 60 cents. Where else can you get such a nifty bargain!?

Knowing your bracket will help you to determine whether many, some, or any of the following strategies will work for you. Warning: Most of them require you to keep careful records, in case the ever-alert IRS challenges a deduction. When it comes to income taxes, pack rats always pay *less*.

1. Fund your 401(k), IRA, and other tax-deferring retirement plans to the max. (Yes, I've said it before in this book, but remember Ms. West's dictum.)

2. Put money in flexible-spending accounts. Many companies allow employees to contribute pretax earnings to FSAs to pay medical and dependent-care expenses. Such cash escapes federal *and* state tax everywhere except in greedy Pennsylvania and New Jersey. Thus, if your combined federal-and-state tax bracket is 40 percent, every dollar of medical expenses you pay from your FSA costs you only 60 cents on an after-tax basis. It gets better: You and a working spouse can *each* fund medical-care FSAs and dependent-care FSAs.

3. Buy tax-exempt bonds. They're issued by states, cities, and other governmental units, and they're free of federal taxes. Thus, a top-rated municipal bond ("muni bond") paying 5.65 percent would be the equivalent of a corporate bond with a 8.19 percent taxable yield if you are in the 31 percent federal bracket. If you live in the state where the muni bond was issued, its interest payments will be free of state tax as well. (I challenge you to find a *safe* investment paying more in real terms than a high-rated muni bond.)

4. Invest in U.S. Savings Bonds. Your interest is exempt from state and local levies, and you won't owe federal tax until you redeem the bonds. If you use the money to pay college tuition, you may not have to pay any tax on the interest. (This break depends on your age, your income, and whose tuition you pay.)

5. Take deductions for charitable work. If you do volunteer work for a church, a synagogue, or a charitable organization, you can deduct 14 cents a mile for travel to and from meetings, fund-raisers, and other events. You also can deduct parking fees and tolls, as well as bus, train, and taxi fares and out-of-pocket expenses—say, for phone calls, stationery, and stamps.

6. Give money and other assets to your children—within the legal limits. This reduces the size of your estate and shields the gifts from estate taxes, which could be up to 55 percent at the federal level alone. You won't trigger gift tax if your annual gifts to any one person don't exceed $10,000 ($20,000 if you and your spouse each make the gift).

In addition to that $10,000 a year, you may give a total of $675,000 tax-free during the course of your lifetime. (This limit will rise gradually to $1 million in 2006.)

7. Make moonlighting pay. If you have self-employment income from consulting or other freelance work, you can usually write off most business expenses—including up to $19,000 a year for tools and equipment, such as computers and software. If you use a room in your home exclusively for business purposes, you can take a home-office deduction. Warning: The IRS has strict restrictions on this write-off. Before taking it, consult a tax pro or IRS Publication 587 for more details.

8. Keep wages in the family. If you are self-employed or have a sideline business, you are entitled to put your children on the payroll. Of course, they must do actual work and can't be paid more than the going rate for the kind of work that they do. You'll then be able to deduct their wages, and the child's standard deduction will shelter $4,300 from tax. Anything above that will be taxed at the child's rate, usually 15 percent. (The stiff kiddie tax on the investment income of children under age 14 doesn't apply to income they earn from jobs.)

9. Get a home-equity loan. Interest on home-equity loans of up to $100,000 is generally tax-deductible, and the borrowed money can be spent for any purpose. Sometimes it makes sense to use such a loan to pay off your credit-card balances, student loans, or car loans; interest on them is not only higher but is not deductible.

10. Take advantage of long-term capital gains rates. You pay regular income taxes on interest and dividends. But you pay no more than 20 percent on profits when you sell investments that you have held for more than a year. As a result, tax-wise investors favor growth stocks over bonds and other securities that throw off sizable amounts of highly taxed income. Many knowledgeable retirees invest for growth and sell a portion of their portfolios each year. They then pay 20 percent on their long-term gains to the IRS, rather than invest for income and pay federal rates of up to 39.6 percent.

11. Reduce your dividend income. If you're planning to sell a stock, do so after a dividend is declared but before it is paid. During that period, the dividend is reflected in the price of the stock, which qualifies for the 20 percent capital gains rate, provided you have owned the investment for at least a year and a day.

12. Open an Education IRA for kids under 18. You can contribute $500 a year to such an account. The contributions aren't deductible, but the earnings aren't taxed if they are used to pay college tuition. You're eligible for the full contribution if your adjusted gross income, with some modifications, is less than $150,000 for couples filing jointly, or less than $95,000 for singles.

For more tax-saving strategies, consult an annual guide such as *J.K. Lasser's Your Income Tax* (Macmillan, $14.95), *The Ernst & Young Tax Guide* (John Wiley & Sons, $15.95), or the Internal Revenue Service's free Publication 17, *Your Federal Income Tax* (call 1-800-TAX-FORM or visit www.irs.gov). You can also try any popular tax software program, like TurboTax/MacInTax from Intuit (for more information, visit www.intuit.com), TaxCut (visit www.taxcut.com), or TaxAct (visit www.taxact.com on the Web).

Beware of Overpaying

Many taxpayers intentionally have so much tax withheld from their paychecks that they are guaranteed a juicy refund. This form of forced saving is just plain dumb. You lose the use of the money, and the Internal Revenue Service doesn't pay interest. In effect, you are lending money to the federal government for free.

A better strategy is to make a close estimate of what your tax bill will likely be and pay accordingly, either through payroll withholding or with quarterly estimated payments. Your payroll office at work, a tax accountant, or a computer tax program can help you make an accurate estimate. To avoid penalty, your estimate must generally equal at least 90 percent of your tax obligation or 100 percent of what you paid the previous year.

HEAD OFF THE DREADED AMT

If anything ever demonstrated the law of unintended consequences, it's the alternative minimum tax—commonly known as the *dreaded* alternative minimum tax. The AMT is the extra tax that more than 800,000 unfortunate folks have to pay, on top of their regular income tax. It was originally enacted by Congress in 1969 to prevent seven-digit fat cats from using sophisticated shelters and slick dodges to pay no income tax at all. Trouble is, the AMT has morphed into something that also hits and hurts a large and growing number of middle-income people whose only offense is that they have a significant amount of legitimate tax deductions and credits.

The number of the deductions and credits that are subject to the AMT has been fast expanding. The Congressional Joint Committee on Taxation expects that the number of people subject to the AMT will zoom to 8.4 million by the year 2007. Thus, you'd do well to check with a tax pro: Are you in danger of being afflicted with the AMT? If you are, you may be able to take some steps, before year-end, to either escape it or soften its blow.

Basically, here's how the complex AMT works.

You (or your tax pro) calculate (or estimate) your federal income tax at the regular rates, which range from 15 percent to 39.6 percent of your adjusted gross income. Then, in a second maneuver, you compute your tax using AMT rates, which start at 26 percent and climb to 28 percent on taxable incomes of $175,000 or more. You have to pay whichever tax is *steeper.*

The *Fairmark Press Tax Guide for Investors* cites this example. Say that your regular income tax is $47,000. But when you calculate your tax using the AMT rules, you come up with $58,000. You have to pay $11,000 of AMT in addition to the $47,000 of regular income tax.

The AMT is often higher than your regular income tax because the AMT disallows many of the most important tax deductions, exemptions, and credits that you would normally take.

Among the things *not* allowed by the AMT are:

- The exemptions you claim for yourself, your spouse, and your dependents.
- State and local income taxes and property taxes.
- Profits from incentive stock options that you exercise and sell in the same year (qualified stock options are not subject to the AMT).
- Medical expenses (under 10 percent of your AGI).
- Certain miscellaneous deductions.
- Interest expenses on home-equity loans and some other real estate loans.
- Investment interest expenses.
- Many other tax credits that you are allowed to take on your regular return.

What you can do to head off the AMT is very limited. However, it may help for you to reverse the usual year-end tax strategy and, instead, choose to collect all the income you can this year and defer, until next year, taking as many deductions as you can. The choices are complex, and you may well need the help of a tax pro who thoroughly understands the nuances of the AMT.

Some good news: You may be able to apply part or all of your AMT liability to trim the tax you pay in future years. Ask your tax preparer if you qualify for the so-called AMT credit carry-forward.

Cut Your Taxes by Giving Money to Your Kids

Want to make sure your kids have a comfortable retirement? When each is born, invest $10,000 in a tax-deferred account. In 65 years, the money will grow to $6.6 million, assuming that it compounds at 11 percent a year. That percentage is the average return for large-company stocks during the past seven decades. Even assuming that inflation drops to an unusually low 3 percent a year, each child's nest egg will be worth just under $1 million in today's dollars by the time he or she reaches retirement age.

We're only half joking. Yes, when most children are born, their parents don't have a spare $10,000 to invest for them. Moreover, only one tax-deferred investment is available to children—unless they earn money from jobs, perhaps as actors or models. In that case, their parents or guardians can open IRAs, Keoghs, or other tax-advantaged retirement accounts for them. (I explain the single exception at the end of this Week 13 chapter.)

There are three persuasive reasons to give money to your kids and invest it for them throughout their childhood years:

1. They'll pay lower taxes on the earnings than you would.
2. You'll be moving money out of your estate so that, if you die prematurely, that money can't be taxed.
3. You're piling up the cash you'll eventually need to send your kids to college or perhaps give them a head start on their careers.

Depending on your circumstances, there may be powerful reasons *not* to give money to your kids. More about that later. Meanwhile, here are two basic rules to keep in mind:

1. You can't give a child more than $10,000 a year— $20,000 if you make the gift jointly with your spouse—without triggering gift taxes. If you do make a gift that exceeds $10,000 (or $20,000 jointly), be sure to file Form 709 with that year's tax return, to head off any problems for you, or your heirs, with the Internal Revenue Service.
2. If your child is under 18—under 21, in some states— don't give the money directly to him or her. Minors aren't allowed to execute contracts, so they can't invest money or even withdraw it—say, from a savings account. You can get such a gift *out of* a savings or investment account only by going to court and asking a judge to appoint you as your child's financial guardian. Then you can act on his or her behalf.

To avoid this hassle, you can open a custodial account for a child at any bank, brokerage, or mutual fund company.

This is where you park your gifts for the child, plus his or her earnings from the account. All you need is a Social Security number for the child.

Depending on your state, the account is known as either an UGMA (for Uniform Gift to Minors Act) or an UTMA (for Uniform Transfers to Minors Act). You can appoint yourself as custodian but, depending on your age and health, you might prefer to name someone else. Reason: If the custodian dies, assets in the UGMA or UTMA may be taxed in his or her estate.

Now, here are two reasons that you might want to put money in a child's name:

1. *You'll save on taxes.* If your child is under age 14, the first $700 in annual investment earnings isn't subject to federal income tax, and the next $700 is taxed at the child's rate, presumably 15 percent. Investment earnings above $1,400 are taxed at the parents' rate.

   The savings can be significant. On $1,400 of interest income, a child in the 15 percent bracket would pay only $105 in federal taxes. But a parent would pay $392 in federal taxes if he or she were in the 28 percent tax bracket, and $554 if in the top 39.6 percent bracket. (This assumes that the income is not long-term capital gains, which are taxed at a maximum 20 percent.)

   It gets better when your child is older than age 14. All of his or her interest, dividends, and capital gains are then taxed at the child's rate, not the parents' rate.

2. *You can spend the money on the child for almost any purpose.* Don't misunderstand. You'll lose the tax break if you spend the child's money on something frivolous or marginal, like a trip to Walt Disney World, or on anything that constitutes an ordinary parental obligation, such as clothing, food, or shelter. But you can spend the money on anything special that benefits the child: private school, college, summer camp, music lessons, and so on. By using custodial accounts, you reduce your taxes on the earnings on money that you would have set aside anyway for these purposes. You avoid paying for them out of highly taxed current income.

Why wouldn't every parent rush to open custodial accounts for his or her children? Because of these two major disadvantages to custodial accounts:

1. At age 18 (or 21, in some states), your child will reach majority and will automatically get control of the assets in a custodial account. Your gifts to the account are irrevocable. There's no legal step you can take if your child decides to spend his or her college savings on a car or a cult. Fortunately, you don't have to let this concern stop you from transferring assets to your children. If you're worried about what they will do with the money when they turn 18 (or 21), you can stash it in an irrevocable trust that spells out the conditions under which the children can withdraw funds. A lawyer will set up a trust for $750 to $2,000.
2. A big custodial account in your child's name may reduce the need-based college financial aid for which

he or she may be eligible. Most colleges use an aid formula that requires a dependent child to contribute at least 35 percent of his or her assets to college costs each year. Parents need contribute only 5.6 percent of their assets. So, if you think it's likely that your children will qualify for need-based aid—as opposed to scholarships for scholastic achievement or athletic prowess—save and invest in your own name. For example, you might buy U.S. Savings Bonds. Some or all of the interest will be tax-free if it is spent on college bills and if your income (with your spouse) totals $81,100 or less ($54,100 or less if you are single).

The best strategy with custodial accounts—assuming you are accumulating money to send a child to college—is to concentrate initially on high-growth, low-income investments, such as long-term growth funds. You might, for example, choose Vanguard Index 500 (phone 1-800-662-7447; www.vanguard.com), which mimics the performance of the Standard & Poor's 500 stock index and, in the 1990s, outpaced most mutual funds that concentrated on large-company stocks.

When your child is within seven years of entering college, gradually switch your emphasis to low-risk, income-generating investments, such as certificates of deposit, money market mutual funds, and short-term bond funds. Another popular choice is U.S. Treasury bonds timed to mature when your son or daughter is ready to go to college. If your child's college fund still falls short of the total bill, you might give him or her highly appreciated securities. Then, when your child sells them, they'll be taxed at his or her low rate. Of course, you must stick within the annual $10,000 gift limit—$20,000 if you make the gift jointly with your spouse. For more on how to save for college wisely, read Week 25: Choose the Right Investment Mix.

What about the tax-deferred investment we mentioned earlier? If you've read Week 48: Beware the Lure of Tax-Deferred Annuities, you're in for a surprise. It's a variable annuity; it can be invested in stocks, bonds, money market funds, or a combination of them. We have serious reservations about annuities as an investment for you, mostly because of their stiff fees. But a variable annuity can be an excellent choice for a child because:

1. You don't have to worry about surrender charges; the child won't be making premature withdrawals.
2. The child will hold the annuity long enough for earnings to overcome the drag of high fees.

You can be more aggressive with a young child than you would be with yourself. The child—particularly a newborn—will have more than enough time to ride out rocky periods in the stock market.

If you simply don't like annuities, invest the child's money in index funds, such as the Vanguard Index 500. Based on returns in the 1990s, your investment will beat most managed funds and will lose less to taxes. Why? Because index funds trade holdings only to keep their portfolios in line with the indexes they mimic. Thus, capital gains distributions are low, which means less money goes to the IRS and more keeps on compounding.

MAKE A GIFT THAT KEEPS ON GIVING

You can give money directly to a child who is too old for a custodial account (18 or 21, depending on the state). You also can help that child, or a younger one, to build up a tax-advantaged cache for the future. The strategy: Reimburse the child for his or her contributions to an IRA, a 401(k), or another tax-deferred retirement account.

Let's say your granddaughter earns $2,000 as a waitress at a summer resort during each of her four years at college. She needs the money for expenses. Urge her to put the money into an IRA, and give her an equal amount for her expenses.

Result: Assuming big stocks' historic 11 percent annual return, her account will grow to $835,869 by the time she turns 65. And if the savings habit catches on and she continues making $2,000 yearly contributions to the account, she'll have $2.5 million socked away by age 65.

Help Your Child Build
a Roth IRA Fortune

Here's another gift that you can give to your children that stands to grow and grow.

Randy Siller is the regional CEO of Sagemark Consulting, an estate and financial planning firm in Tarrytown, New York (phone 1-914-333-0064). He recommends that parents of fairly young children set up a retirement fund for each of their kids. That's right, a *retirement* fund, one that won't pay off for many years—but then may pay off really big indeed.

What you do is this:

Create a job for your child—perhaps in your own business if you have one, or at home as, say, a computer tutor or file keeper—and pay him or her a realistic wage.

"Let's say," explains Siller, "I have a child who is ten years old. Children today are doing amazing things with computers and with all kinds of work. Let's also say that by working for me in the summer or on weekends during the school year, I could justify paying him or her a couple of thousand dollars a year. Then the child could set up his or her own Roth IRA with that earned income.

"Let's say I do this for ten years, paying him or her $2,000 a year, until the child is 20. Then no more contributions are made to the Roth IRA.

"Let's say that the money grows 10 percent a year. When the child reaches age $59\frac{1}{2}$, that $2,000 a year for ten years will have grown to $1,375,000—and all of it will be available to the child totally tax-free."

That's because, with a Roth IRA, the government does not tax the annual growth on the money, nor does it tax the ultimate distribution of funds. "So," as Siller says, "by the time of the child's retirement, I've subsidized him or her by about one-million-four—which then will buy you maybe a cup of coffee—but one-million-four is one-million-four. At age 59½, the child could take it out and do what he or she wants with it. Or, better yet, if the money is still earning a rate of 10 percent, he or she could take out pieces of it every year, and there would be no income tax, no 10 percent penalty, no tax at all. Not a bad little supplement for your child's retirement."

There are, of course, some important caveats. "Your child needs to do legitimate work. And the wage you pay him or her must be fair and legitimate. You cannot overpay. And you should keep solid records of when and where the child works, what jobs he or she does. You might want to keep time sheets. And if an IRS inspector ever asks one of your employees, he or she should be able to substantiate the records.

"There's still another reason this is a good idea," says Siller. "We try to help our children, but we don't want to overwhelm them with too many gifts during their working years. We don't want to take away their incentive, their desire to work. There's no danger of that by paying them $2,000 a year. But, just think what a Roth IRA could do when your child ultimately reaches retirement!"

For further information, see Chapter 43: Open an IRA—or a Roth IRA.

Beware of the Limits
on Generosity

You'd think it would be the easiest thing in the world to
get rid of your money and make significant gifts to your
family and friends. Well, with one big exception, gifting is
not without limits. Uncle Sam imposes firm restrictions on
the amounts of money, property, stocks, or other assets that
you can give to other people.

Let's start with the exception: The sky's the ceiling
when gifting to your beloved spouse. But not to anyone
else—not to your best pal, not to your live-in lover, certainly
not to your kids.

Beyond the spousal exception, the feds lay on two
basic rules.

Rule 1

You may give up to $10,000 a year—*every* year—to each of
as many individuals as you wish. If you have 10 children,

you can give each of them as much as $10,000 this year and about $10,000 next year, and so on and on. The recipients need not be your kids, or any relative at all. You can give money or other assets to friends or anyone else.

But if you exceed those limits, you have to pay a hefty gift tax, starting at 37 percent and rising to 55 percent for gifts totaling more than $3,000,000.

To elaborate: You can give each child or grandchild—or any other individual, even someone who is not a family member—up to $10,000 a year without running into federal gift taxes. Couples can give up to $20,000 a year to each of an unlimited number of persons.

For example, you might want to give away $10,000 to each of your three children, $10,000 to each of your four grandchildren, and $10,000 to each of your two daughters-in-law and one son-in-law—$100,000 in all. If your spouse matches your gifts, the total would be $200,000.

That certainly would be an unusual burst of generosity. But, if you are a very affluent person, such annual gifts can make sense. They reduce the size of your estate—and the estate taxes that your heirs will have to pay—later on.

You cannot skip one year and double-up in the next. If you don't give someone $10,000 in 2001, you cannot give him or her $20,000 in 2002—only $10,000. This is another case of use it or lose it.

The $10,000 annual limit is set to go up with inflaion, but so far prices have not risen enough to trigger an adjustment.

Rule 2

In addition to the $10,000 per person per year, you may give away a *total* of up to $675,000 in the course of your lifetime to any person—or number of persons. You can give that amount in one lump sum or, more likely, in pieces over the years.

Say you have two children. At some point, you want to give them as much as you can without incurring a gift tax. In that case, you could give each one $337,500 from your lifetime limit—above and beyond the $10,000 annual limit.

The $675,000 lifetime limit will remain in place through 2001. Then, beginning in 2002, it will rise in annual stages to a maximum of $1,000,000 in 2006—unless Congress mandates a change.

Both the U.S. Senate and the House of Representatives have passed a bill to phase out the estate and gift tax over 10 years. As of this writing, the bill has been blocked by outgoing President Bill Clinton's promise to veto it. My own guess is that the feds will not eliminate the tax but will liberalize it, possibly by raising the lifetime limit to $1,000,000 in 2002 or 2003 instead of 2006. So, stick around. You may be able to give still more.

Teach Your Kids About Money

If you have children age 6 years or older, it's time to start teaching them the basics of money and finance.

You should, of course, put the kids on a regular weekly allowance (with modest bonuses for special chores performed) and work out a budget for their spending, saving, and investing. And, at what you think is the proper moment, you should start discussing family financial choices with them. Says Charlotte Baechur, editor of *Zillions,* the Consumers Union magazine for kids: "Parents should be open about money with their children. If they are going to make a purchase that is visible to the child, such as a car or a TV, they should talk about the expense and say things like, 'well, if we buy this, we can't buy that, or we will have to cut back on that.'"

Start giving stocks, savings bonds, and other assets to children for birthday or holiday presents. Suggest to doting grandparents, other relatives, and grown-up family friends that they do the same.

It might seem logical to buy shares of mutual funds, but kids tend to grasp—and learn more from—the ups and downs of specific companies better than those of multi-flavored funds. When buying stocks, it often helps to choose companies that the children might easily relate to, such as Wrigley, Disney, or McDonald's.

Fortunately, you can get a lot of well-produced assistance—from brokerage houses, mutual funds, public service outfits, and others—in teaching your children. In the past several years, there has been a surge of websites devoted to the subject, as well as summer camps, seminars, publications, and so on. What follows is a sampling of the better sources.

The Internet

Many sites can help kids of all ages learn about money and investing. Here are some suggestions for particular age groups.

Ages 6 to 9 years:

- www.fleetkids.com. Sponsored by the Fleet Bank, this site has great games—like "Buy lo, Sell hi" and "Chunka Change"—that teach kids about spending and saving. Children can compete for prizes such as computers and backpacks for their schools.

Ages 10 to 13 years:

- www.strongkids.com. This teaches children about investing, earning, and saving money; it also explains

IRAs, trust funds, and savings accounts for kids under the Uniform Gift to Minors Act. Children can use the "ladder" to chart their savings goals and the "tape measure" to learn about compound interest. The "hard hat quiz" tells them the basics of mutual funds. The site has a thorough glossary of financial terms.

- www.zillions.org. For years, *Zillions* was the premier financial education periodical for children. The printed magazine has since folded, but a website was being built and was scheduled to be in operation late in 2000.

- www.savvystudent.com gives lessons in saving and spending money for entertainment, food, travel, and clothes. Kids can subscribe to a free monthly E-newsletter and use the "Dear Savvy Student" center to submit financial questions online.

Ages 14 to 18 years:

- www.steinroe.com. Sponsored by the investment company of SteinRoe and Farnham in Chicago, this site offers a mutual fund designed especially for kids. Called the SteinRoe Young Investor Fund, it invests in companies that kids tend to know something about: Apple, Cisco, General Electric, Microsoft, and others. It has a four-star rating from Morningstar, and for the five year-period through June 2000, the fund returned an average of 25.51 percent. You need a $100 minimum to start and at least $50 a month after that.

- www.youngbiz.com. This stimulating site tracks the performance of stocks that teens are familiar with: Coca-Cola, Pepsi, McDonald's, and Disney. It also has fascinating articles about student investors and student-run businesses, as well as career planning advice.
- www.ssa.gov/kids/faq.html. One of many good sites presented by U.S. Government agencies, this one tells visitors just about all they would want to know about the Social Security system.

For parents:

- www.kidsmoney.org. This site is replete with articles on how parents can teach kids about money; it also has a section where parents vote on the most important principles about money to impress upon children. There are many suggestions for ways kids can make money, such as taking pictures at parties, typing papers, and raking leaves.

Newspapers

The Wall Street Journal Classroom Edition is a comprehensive program sent directly to classrooms for $165 a year. Each month during the academic year (September through May), 30 copies of a 24-page, four-color *Wall Street Journal* classroom edition are sent to a schoolroom. In addition, the teacher gets one subscription to the regular daily *WSJ*. The well-edited monthly edition, directed at middle-school and high-school students, has domestic and international stories about enterprise, careers, technology, marketing, investment, and more. To order, call 1-800-544-0522. A tip: Schools often enlist parents or local businesspeople to sponsor subscriptions. The edition also offers optional quarterly videos produced by CNBC. Topics are drawn from the monthly paper.

Summer Camps

- Camp Start-up, run by Independent Means Inc., based in Santa Barbara, CA, has a two-week program in which girls ages 13 to 18 create faux enterprises and hear talks by accomplished businesswomen. Cost: $1,600. Phone 1-800-350-1816, Web www.dollardiva.com.
- Millennium Entrepreneurs, based in Chula Vista, CA, offers one- to three-week sessions at places from Hawaii to Washington, DC, for boys and girls ages 8 years and older. They study the stock market, manage checking accounts for their spending money, and learn financial basics. Cost: $850 to $2,550. Phone: 1-619-476-7655.
- American Computer Experience offers computer camps at 75 universities. Campers, ages 7 to 16 years, learn how to program, build a website, and run software applications. Sessions cost $525 to $895. Call 1-800-386-4223.

Dozens of other camps are listed on www.kidscamps. com under **business camps**.

Brokerage Houses

Merrill Lynch offers a load of free materials for teens, including lively comic books ("Savin' Dave and the Compounders"), brochures ("Ten Ways to Talk with Your Teens about Money"), pocket quizzes about money matters, and much more (go to www.plan.ml.com/education/familysavings/index.html on the Web). Similar valuable packages are produced by Morgan Stanley Dean Witter (phone Bret Gallaway: 1-212-762-7843) and by many other brokerages.

Share Your Financial Basics with Your Mate

It's amazing how loving couples who share so much intimacy in other arenas are often shy and secretive when it comes to talking with each other about their personal finances. Some partners would rather share a toothbrush than a bank account. But keeping a mate in ignorance can be dangerous to your wealth.

Surely you should reveal and explain your finances just before you marry, and then regularly go over them at least once a year. This week is a good time to review your assets.

Start by making updated lists of all the valuable possessions you own separately or in common. You should know the names, addresses, and phone and fax numbers of the financial professionals in your mate's life. They include any stockbroker, accountant, personal banker, attorney, insurance agent, and financial planner he or she uses.

In the lists of your assets, include all real estate, bank and brokerage accounts, cars and boats, precious jewelry, works of art, and insurance policies. Keep the separate and joint lists of your assets in the same secure place where you store your wills.

You also should learn the details of your spouse's job benefits and work history, such as whether you have survivor's rights to his or her pension. If your mate held a previous job long enough to earn a pension, you could be eligible for additional retirement funds.

Past military service often endows survivors with financial rights in the event of a spouse's death. If your husband or wife was in the armed forces, you might be eligible for G.I. life insurance, a pension, burial expenses, and even a Department of Veterans Affairs mortgage loan. To apply for these benefits, you will need the veteran's discharge papers.

Rent *two* safe-deposit boxes. Put in your own box all the papers you will need if your spouse dies. These should include copies of just about all the documents mentioned above. Banks in many states seal the box of the deceased upon notification of death, and you may have to wait weeks or months for a court to grant permission to open your mate's box. Also leave copies of all necessary documents with your lawyer, and with at least one adult child or some other trusted third party.

Both spouses should know where both the originals and copies of other valuable documents are kept, including birth certificates, marriage license, and insurance policies.

When you take inventory of your separate assets and liabilities, decide what property you want to continue to keep in your own name and what you want to merge. Many financial advisers suggest that you keep separate as well as joint bank accounts.

Be sure to familiarize yourself with the law. Each state has its own laws governing marital and separate property, and stipulating what happens if the two are mingled. One tip: If you want to put property in your spouse's name, federal law allows you to transfer an unlimited amount without paying gift or estate taxes.

You and your spouse should discuss the advantages and disadvantages of various forms of joint ownership. An accountant, lawyer, or certified financial planner can explain the nuances. For example, in one form of joint ownership, the title specifies that if one of you dies, the property goes automatically to the spouse. In another form, however, each of you owns half of the property, and you can leave your share to whomever you wish, such as a child from an earlier marriage. If a married couple takes title to a house as tenants in common, then either partner can leave his or her share of the house to whomever he or she names in his or her will.

What about the financial rights of two people living together without benefit of clergy? Alas, the law is often muddy. Take inheritance, for example. When one member of a married couple dies without a will, state laws typically ensure that the bulk of the person's property will pass to the surviving spouse. But when an unmarried person leaves no will, all of his or her earthly goods can be claimed by the next of kin. Even a loathsome great-aunt thousands of miles away stands before a live-in partner in the inheritance line.

The message is clear: If you are living with someone to whom you eventually want to will some or all of your worldly goods, you had better put your intentions in writing—in an unshakable will that has been drafted by a lawyer, legally signed, and properly witnessed. That may sound unromantic, but the stark reality is: Putting your financial intentions in writing is the best way to protect a joint venture of the heart.

Written contracts can protect your interest if disputes arise with your business partners—or with an ex-spouse or government authorities—over such matters as insurance, inheritance, or debts that you have to pay.

Unmarried long-term partners should do the following:

- Name your partner as a beneficiary of your life insurance policy.
- Buy medical insurance if either partner isn't covered by a group health plan.
- Sign a medical power-of-attorney permitting your partner to visit you and to make medical decisions if you're seriously ill.
- Perhaps most important, write a will so that you can leave to your partner what you want him or her to have.

Couples with little money or other assets might get by with the fill-in-the-blanks legal forms for creating wills found in some books on living together. If your finances are fuller or more complicated, you need a lawyer's assistance to draw up a financial agreement. If you choose to do it yourself, your agreement at least should be notarized and checked hard to make sure it doesn't contain a mistake that could invalidate it. Contracts between unmarried couples generally are recognized by the courts as long as they violate no laws and both partners enter into them freely. For more about wills, see Week 39: Write a Will That Works.

Unmarried couples should own things separately. For example, he buys and owns the car, she buys and owns the computer—though both partners use them. Unwed partners also should acquire as little as possible together and keep receipts or other records of what each buys. Doing that will prevent bitter battles if and when they split up.

For much the same reason, unmarried couples should not have joint bank accounts or credit cards. Generally, in joint charge accounts, each person is 100 percent responsible for debts incurred by the other. Creditors who may be chasing one of the two partners can seize assets in joint bank accounts.

The tidiest way to split household expenses is down the middle. An exception occurs, of course, if one partner is enrolled full-time in college or is too ill to work. The other, working partner then pays the bills, but records should be kept. Ultimately, he or she should be paid back, at least in part.

You and your unmarried partner may well save money by filing your taxes separately instead of jointly, thus escaping the notorious marriage penalty. But that saving will be minuscule compared with the bigger hit that you—or rather, your heirs—stand to take on estate taxes. To hold down those taxes, the more affluent partner may choose to give annual cash gifts to the less affluent partner.

Married partners can give unlimited gifts to each other without paying any federal or state gift tax. Similarly, upon death, married partners can pass all their assets to each other, free of estate taxes. Unmarried partners cannot. Their gifts are limited to $10,000 annually to each of any number of individuals, plus $675,000 in the course of a lifetime. Any amount above those ceilings stands to be slapped with federal and state gift or estate taxes. One creative way to get around at least part of this is to buy life insurance—and make your partner both the owner and the beneficiary of the policy.

For more gifting rules, see Week 14: Beware of the Limits on Generosity.

Improve Your Credit Record

To manage your personal finances smoothly, you need a clean credit record—a sterling history of paying your bills fully and on time. Such a record will make it easier to obtain a mortgage or other loan, a lease on an apartment, a credit card, a hotel reservation, and even a job. This week, find out what your credit rating is now, how to improve it, and how to repair your record if you've damaged it—perhaps as a result of youthful oversplurging on credit cards or something more serious, such as a job loss or a debilitating illness.

Start by checking up on your record, which is based on your bill-paying history and on information you've provided when applying for credit—say, for a charge account or a credit card. You'll recall that card applications ask for your age, income, employment, length of residence in your community, and other details about your personal and financial life. Your prospective creditors send this information to one or more of the three major credit bureaus and perhaps to local ones as well. The trouble is, errors can easily creep into these records, perhaps because your name is similar to someone else's, or a clerk has made a mistake in entering your Social Security number. A Consumers Union review of credit reports found that 48 percent were inaccurate in some way—nearly 20 percent were so seriously flawed that the victim could have had trouble.

Best advice: Double-check your credit record once a year. Don't wait until a mistake leads to an unpleasant surprise—for example, you're denied credit, a lease, or a job. Begin by calling all three national credit bureaus, because you don't know which ones your potential landlord, employer, or creditors use. They are:

- Equifax (Phone: 1-800-685-1111; Web: www.equifax .com).
- Experian (Phone: 1-888-EXPERIAN; Web: www .experian.com).
- Trans Union (Phone: 1-800-888-4213; Web: www .transunion.com).

All three companies are required to send you a free copy of your report if you have been denied credit or turned down for an apartment or bank account because of your credit rating. Otherwise, fees for credit reports vary by state, but are typically under $10.

You might also ask your bank or a local retailer for the names of credit bureaus that serve your area. Phone them to find out how to get their records of your credit history.

When you receive the reports, you most likely will find them far from complete because they contain, primarily, information supplied by mortgage lenders, issuers of bank cards (such as MasterCard and Visa), and travel and entertainment cards and charge accounts at national department stores. Your reports won't reflect most of the bills you pay, such as those from utility companies, your landlord, your doctor, and your dentist.

Read the reports to make sure the information—however incomplete—is accurate.

How to Correct Errors in Your Credit Record

What should you do if you find information in a report that you think is inaccurate or unfair? First, write to the creditor who complained about you. Insist that the record be corrected. Then, write to the credit bureau and request that it get the correct information from the creditor.

You can challenge any information in your file. If the credit bureau cannot confirm the disputed information, it must delete it. At your request, the bureau must also send a revised copy of your report to anyone who has sought credit information on you in the past six months. You may also ask the credit bureau to send a correction to any employer who has received a credit report on you within the past two years. It's important to clear the record because any complaints from creditors, or any other negative information, can stay in your report for seven years (10 years, if you go bankrupt).

Even if the credit bureau finds that its information is valid, you can write an explanation—make sure it's fewer than 100 words—for anything you may have done that is tarnishing your record. The bureau must then attach your explanation, or a summary of it, to your report. In that way, anyone who receives your credit history in the future will also get your side of the story. If you ask, the bureau will also send copies of your explanation to anyone who requested your credit report in the past six months or to any employer who requested it in the past two years.

A few months after you've corrected any errors—or asked a credit bureau to attach your statement to a blemished report—write away for an updated copy of your credit record. It'll cost you no more than another $10, but that's a modest enough investment if you discover that the mistake hasn't been corrected or your explanatory statement hasn't been attached to your report.

How to Repair a Bad Credit Rating

If your record is poor because you've been tardy when paying bills, cleaning it up becomes tougher. Don't make the mistake of hiring a credit repair service, also known as a credit doctor or credit clinic. For $500 or so, it will promise to purge negative information about you from your report and even get you a credit card. Actually, these firms do nothing that you can't do yourself.

Begin by identifying the problem—and then fix it. Even if you are making at least the minimum monthly payments on your debts, creditors will regard you as over your head when 30 to 35 percent of your gross income goes to paying off current debts, including a home mortgage.

If you've been turned down for a credit card, ask the card issuer for the reason. If it's because your credit rating is subpar, consider asking a bank to give you a secured credit card. You'll have to deposit a minimum amount—say,

$2,000—in a savings account as collateral, to ensure that you meet your monthly payments. After 18 months or so of paying your bills on time, you can probably switch to an unsecured card. As an alternative to a secured card, you may be able to get gasoline or department store charge cards, which are usually easier to obtain than credit cards. Then, pay your bills faithfully, to rebuild your reputation for dependability.

After you've brought your bills and debts under control, notify the credit bureaus. Ask them to attach a statement from you—again, fewer than 100 words—to your file. Be cautious about how you explain the reason for your credit problems; your statement will be read by prospective creditors and employers. For instance, you may not want them to know that you were fired from your last job or that you missed six months of work because of illness.

As you establish a record of paying your bills faithfully, creditors will be more inclined to approve your applications. To be sure they know about your record, you might attach an explanation to each application—just to offset the impact of your unfavorable credit report.

After seven years of keeping your debt-slate clean (10 years in a case of bankruptcy), the blemishes will be removed from your record.

How to Improve Your Credit Rating

Regardless of whether your credit record has been virginal, you'll find it advantageous to take steps to raise your rating. Most lenders use computerized credit-scoring systems to decide whether to accept applications for credit and charge cards, and for loans. These systems take into account a broad range of characteristics that you can't control, such as your age, or how long you've held your job or owned your home. (If you've changed jobs or moved within the past two years, you might attach an explanation to your application.) It's therefore crucial to improve your record on the characteristics you *can* control. Take these steps:

- *Pay your bills on time.* Sounds obvious, but this is the single most important move you can make. Lenders reckon that how you've paid in the past indicates how you'll pay in the future. In addition, keep a tight rein on your borrowing so that debt payments don't exceed the threshold mentioned earlier—30 to 35 percent of your gross income.

- *Hold no more than four credit or charge cards.* Potential lenders look at the number of cards you have and total up the unsecured credit available on them. If a lender deems the maximum more than you can safely carry, your application will be turned down. Don't just cut up your unnecessary cards; the accounts will still show up on your record. Instead, write or call the card issuers to cancel your accounts and ask that the credit bureaus be notified that they were in good standing when you canceled them.

- *Don't max out on the cards you keep.* You risk being rejected, for instance, if you owe 80 percent of your credit limits on two or more cards. Be cautious about carrying balances on plastic.

- *Avoid loans from finance companies.* Lenders don't like to see them on credit records because a sizable percentage of bad credit risks have been in debt to these outfits. If your payment record on such loans is good, however, you may not lose points.

• *Don't submit loan applications to too many lenders.* Every time you apply, the lender checks your credit history and the inquiry is recorded by the credit bureau. If you submit applications to several lenders while hunting for a loan, this can be misinterpreted— for example, by a credit-card issuer—as evidence that you are trying to take on too much debt. Best advice: Do your loan shopping by phone, and then submit a single application for the one you want.

If you don't have a credit history—perhaps because you've just graduated from college, you're recently widowed, or you're a new immigrant—the following moves can help you start establishing one:

• Open and use checking and savings accounts.
• Join a credit union where you work.
• Take out and use a secured credit card or a gasoline or department store charge card.

Then, as explained earlier, build a long-term record of regularly paying your bills—the best sign that you're a creditworthy consumer.

Control Your Debt

Of all the financial mistakes imaginable, the toughest is to fall too deeply into debt. Fortunately, there are ways to figure out how much debt you can comfortably handle. If you take better control of your debts, you can save hundreds of dollars a year—or perhaps thousands. This is the week to do that. Next week, we will follow up with borrowing sensibly.

Here's a quick, two-part test to help determine how much debt is too much for you:

1. Estimate your annual disposable income—that is, all your income, minus your tax withheld and your contributions to various personal retirement, savings, and investment plans.

2. Map out the year's expenses. Calculate how many of them will require various forms of debt—notably, installment loans.

With your net-worth and cash-flow statements in hand, add up all your debts, including your credit-card balances. Then divide the total by your annual disposable income—all your income for the past 12 months, minus taxes, savings and investments, and contributions to retirement plans. The result will indicate how much debt you can afford to carry. Debt counselors and credit managers warn that no more than 15 percent of your disposable income should be committed to installment debt, not counting home-mortgage payments. If you're the sole breadwinner in your family, the recommended limit is 10 percent, unless you have substantial income and don't expect to take on new loans. Your debt payments, *including your mortgage,* should not top 30 to 35 percent of your gross income.

How do you know whether you're courting debt disaster? The National Foundation for Credit Counseling suggests you ask yourself the following questions:

- Are you borrowing for items you used to buy with cash?
- Are you taking out new loans before you pay off your previous loans?
- Are your monthly installment bills, besides rent or mortgage, more than 15 percent of your take-home pay?
- Are creditors threatening to repossess your car or credit cards, or to take other legal action?
- Are your expenses growing faster than your income?
- Do you dip into your savings to pay your regular bills?
- Is your savings reserve less than three months of your take-home pay?

- Are you approaching the limits of all your credit lines?
- Are you usually late in paying your bills?
- Do you make only minimum payments each month?
- Do you find it hard to save at least 10 percent of your take-home pay?
- Are you borrowing from one lender to pay another?
- Do you regularly dip into your checking overdraft?
- Are you using credit cards for items you used to buy with cash?
- Do lenders require a friend or relative to co-sign your loans?
- Are you unable to say how much money you owe?

If you answered yes to any of these questions, you may be headed for debt disaster.

Other signs of danger are obvious if a potential lender denies you credit.

If you tumble too deeply into debt, or you face other credit problems, you *can* get help. For aid in creating a budget or a realistic schedule of repayments, call or write to the National Foundation for Credit Counseling in Silver Spring, Maryland. It has nearly 1,000 offices throughout North America. The toll-free number is 1-800-388-CCCS, and their Web address is www.nfcc.org.

The foundation is associated with Consumer Credit Counseling Service (CCCS), which sponsors local nonprofit organizations supported by banks, credit unions, consumer finance companies, and others. CCCS provides credit counseling to anyone who needs it, for a reasonable fee. Its phone is also 1-800-388-CCCS.

A most important step toward a solid credit rating is to use credit cards intelligently. American households, on average, carry a credit card balance of $7,500.

Two pieces of advice: (1) Reduce your credit-card balance, and (2) be sure to know exactly what the interest charge is. Federal law requires credit-card issuers to declare, on all solicitations and applications for cards, the rate they charge, whether it is variable or fixed, and how it is determined.

Some additional money-saving recommendations to cardholders:

- Send in your credit-card payment as soon as you get your bill. The sooner the bank receives it, the less interest you will pay.
- Pay *more* than the minimum payment. If you send in only the minimum amount due, it can take you decades to pay off your balance.
- Refuse a card issuer's offer to make no payment for one month. You'll just dig yourself deeper into debt.

Consolidate your cards. The fewer you hold, the easier it will be to keep track of them. Drop a card that is charging a higher rate in favor of one with a lower rate. But beware of "teaser rates"—very low initial rates that *surge* after a short time.

Now, resolve to pay off your highest-rate loans first. Liquidating a debt carrying an 18 percent rate gives you an automatic tax-free return of 18 percent—at no risk. At the very least, if you've been making only the minimum required payments on your credit-card debts, resolve to pay $50 more per month. According to the Consumer Credit Counseling Service, that small extra amount would enable you to repay a $3,000 credit-card balance in 3 years, versus 8 years if you made only the minimum payments. You would also save $1,800.

Here's another alternative: Get a low-rate credit card and switch your balances to your new account. Or pay off your credit-card debt with a low-rate home-equity loan.

Now, turn to the net-worth and cash-flow statements you drew up in Week 6: Figure Out What You Are Really Worth. Note *all* your debts—including unpaid balances on credit and charge cards—and the rate of interest you are paying on each. Then, list the debts in order of those rates, starting with the highest. Your list will probably look something like this:

- Credit-card balances, 17.36 percent (the average in late September 2000).
- Home-equity loan (if you have one), 10.25 percent.
- Car loan, 9.72 percent (48 months, new car).
- Student loans, 9 percent.
- Home mortgage, 7.92 percent (the average for 30-year fixed-rate loans).

Don't rush to pay off any debt for which the federal government lets you deduct the interest payments on your tax return (e.g., mortgages and home-equity loans). In fact, if those are your only debts, putting your money into savings would be wiser than paying them off early.

When you conclude that you are in trouble, your number-one priority is to cut out all unnecessary costs and drastically step up your debt repayments, starting with your high-cost credit-card balances. Wherever possible, lower your interest charges. If you can't make headway against your debts, don't panic and don't sign up for a consolidation loan; you'll only wind up paying more interest to the lender than you do to your creditors now. Instead, meet with your creditors and ask to restructure your loans—that is, to stretch out your payments or even reduce your debt. The last thing they want is for you to default or go bankrupt.

If you still can't manage your debt, seek help from the nearest nonprofit credit counseling service, which you can find by calling the Consumer Credit Counseling Services (1-800-388-CCCS). A counselor will analyze your finances and try to work out a repayment schedule with your creditors, sometimes stretching for years. The first visit to the counselor is free, and later you'll be charged a modest fee, depending on your ability to pay.

While you're digging your way out of debt, you must continue to save, even if only a token 3 percent to 5 percent of your before-tax income. You simply can't afford to put your financial goals on hold. No matter how straitened your circumstances, you can't delay the two major expenses of middle-income America: paying for your children's education and saving for your own retirement.

Determine a Sensible Policy for Borrowing

Think hard about whether you really want to borrow at all. You'll have to pay steeper interest, in real terms, than you have paid in years. Inflation is low—roughly 3 percent in mid-2000—and one consequence is that the real cost of borrowing is high. Banks are charging close to 17 percent on purchases paid for with credit cards—and often more than that. Subtract the 3 percent inflation rate from the 17 percent interest rate; you're paying a true rate of 14 percent on your credit-card loan. The real rate back in 1980 was only 7 percent! Unlike those days, you cannot count on repaying creditors in the future with significantly cheaper dollars.

Your borrowing is also costlier because your interest payments on your car, college-tuition, credit-card, and other consumer loans are no longer tax-deductible. That increases the financial pressure on you, so consider carefully your many credit choices.

Here's a basic guide to borrowing sensibly:

1. Never borrow more than you can reasonably pay off.
2. Never borrow for luxuries, such as sports cars or jewelry, if that means you will not be able to borrow for necessities, such as mortgage, medical, or education expenses. After necessities, in order of importance, are loans to finance long-term assets such as home improvements, major appliances, and furniture.
3. Be sure to reserve some borrowing capacity for emergencies, such as unforeseen medical bills.

Prudent borrowers keep their debt expenses as low as possible by:

1. Paying as much up front as they can.
2. Applying for the shortest-term loans they can afford.
3. Shopping around for the best borrowing deals.
4. Negotiating rates and fees.

There are much less expensive ways of borrowing than to tap into your credit cards. What are some relatively low-cost sources of credit?

A smart place to start searching for a general-purpose loan is the bank where you have your checking and savings accounts. Many banks charge as much as two percentage points *less* for loans to customers than to noncustomers. You often can get *unsecured* loans, without any collateral, if you have a steady job or other regular income and show that you can afford the repayments. For unsecured loans, banks have been charging about 15.4 percent. That's better than the rates on credit cards, so it may make sense to switch to an unsecured bank-credit line and pay off your plastic.

Credit unions are another font of credit, though few of them make unsecured personal loans larger than $5,000. You can join a credit union by depositing only a nominal sum—typically, $5 to $25. Joining is a lot easier than it used to be; membership now tops 75.4 million. You may be eligible and not even know it. You may not have to work for the same company or belong to the same union or community organization as other members. Some credit unions even permit members' relatives to join. For more information about credit unions in your area, write to Credit Union National Association, P.O. Box 431, Madison, WI 53701. You can reach it on the World Wide Web at www.cuna.org.

Many employers let you borrow from the vested assets that you have put away in a 401(k), 403(b), profit-sharing, or other retirement savings plan. Typically, you can borrow *all* of your vested benefit up to $10,000 from such a plan, and up to *one-half* of your vested benefit between $10,000 and $50,000. Federal restrictions limit the maximum loan to $50,000, and employers must charge the going market rate of interest—usually, one or two percentage points above the prime rate. Your costs for such loans vary from one institution to another but in mid-2000 were around 11 percent. That's a lower rate than you would pay to many commercial lenders. You usually must repay the loan within five years through payroll deductions; 10 years—or, in some cases, up to 25 years—is allowed for repayment of loans to buy or renovate your primary residence. If you leave your job, however, you must repay the money immediately, or you will owe taxes on it plus a 10 percent penalty. The penalty is waived if you are older than $59\frac{1}{2}$.

If you own publicly traded stocks or bonds, or mutual funds, you can go to a stockbroker and take out a margin loan—commonly, for half the value of your securities. You'll generally pay interest of 0.5 to 2 percentage points more than the so-called broker call rate, which was 8.25 percent in mid-2000. Your interest payments, up to an amount equal to your investment income on the loan proceeds, will be tax-deductible, as long as the securities you use as collateral are not tax-exempt. *Warning:* If your securities' value drops, your broker may demand that you put up more securities, or cash, as collateral. If you can't do it, he or she may sell some of your investments. Best advice: Stay on the safe side. Don't borrow more than 20 percent of your portfolio's value.

If you own a whole, universal, or variable life insurance policy, you can borrow the amount of the policy's cash value. You never have to repay the principal, but if you die with the loan outstanding, it will be deducted from the face amount paid to your beneficiaries.

If you borrow from your family, the loan need not be secured by collateral. Of course, in exchange for easy credit, you run the risk of straining a family relationship. To lessen that possibility, draw up a promissory note (many stationery stores sell preprinted forms). You should agree to an annual rate of interest that is high enough to compensate your relatives for their forgone income, and to a regular repayment schedule.

When looking for money, canvass at least a half-dozen lenders; you'll be surprised at how much rates and terms vary on loans. You may also be surprised at how willing lenders are to adjust their rates and terms to make their loans more affordable to you. But don't forget: Lenders are in the business of making loans, just as car dealers earn their living selling autos. Both are usually eager to make deals with creditworthy customers. You can shop for a loan by telephone or on the Internet, but make sure that the rates being quoted are for loans whose terms and conditions are identical in every respect.

Depending on what *type* of loan you need, here are the most desirable places to search.

Real Estate Loans

When financing a house or condo, you will generally get the best rates and terms at savings and loan associations and at mortgage banking firms. (Credit unions usually *don't* offer better deals than other mortgage lenders.) Personal finance magazines typically publish average rates that you can use as benchmarks. In late September 2000, 30-year fixed-rate mortgages averaged 7.92 percent; 15-year fixed mortgages, 7.58 percent; and one-year adjustable-rate mortgages, 7.27 percent (after the first year, the ARM rate often goes up about 2 percentage points).

Home-Equity Loans

Your bank, savings and loan (S&L), or credit union normally is the best source for these loans, as well as loans for major expenses such as home renovations and college tuition, and for consolidation of credit-card debts. In late September 2000, rates on home-equity loans averaged 10.25

percent, and rates on home-equity lines of credit averaged 9.25 percent. Interest payments are tax-deductible on loans of less than $100,000. (Interest payments on loan balances that exceed $100,000 are tax-deductible only if you use the borrowed cash for home improvements, business expenses, or income-generating investments.) You can usually borrow 70 percent to 80 percent of your equity in your home (equity = market value – your mortgage balance). Beware of overusing home-equity financing; if you can't make the payments, you could lose the roof over your head.

Car Loans

As mentioned, your cheapest financing may be a home-equity loan. Be sure, however, to pay it off within three or four years; otherwise, your balance may exceed the value of your depreciated auto. For the same reason, if you are financing your purchase with a car loan, take only one that will be paid off in three to four years. Your best sources for the loan may be your bank, S&L, credit union—or the dealer. Today, dealers provide financing for nearly 80 percent of the cars they sell.

College Loans

Your college-bound child can borrow directly from the federal government, or from private lenders under the government-guaranteed Stafford loan program. Both sources generally provide up to $5,500 a year for undergraduates and higher amounts for graduate students. Interest rates, capped at a maximum of 8.25 percent, are pegged to the three-month

Treasury bill and reset once a year. Parents can take out PLUS loans (Parent Loans to Undergraduate Students) for as much as their out-of-pocket costs for school bills. PLUS loans also have variable interest rates; they are tied to the one-year Treasury bill rate, reset annually, and are capped at 9 percent. (For more about U.S. Government loans, call 1-800-433-3243, or visit www.studentloans.com for a summary of federal financial aid programs.) You can also use a home-equity loan or a personal loan for college bills.

Personal Loans

Your best source here is most likely the bank, S&L, or credit union where you keep your checking and savings accounts. Personal loans differ from car loans, mortgages, and home-equity loans in one major respect: Personal loans are usually backed only by your promise to repay the debt. Hence, you must pay more for them. Still, the rate is lower than what you typically pay on credit cards, making a personal loan an attractive way to consolidate your plastic debt. You can shave a couple of percentage points off the rate on a personal loan by putting up collateral, such as a savings account, certificates of deposit, or stocks, bonds, or other securities. Typically, you can't take out a personal loan for more than $10,000 from a bank or $5,000 from a credit union, and you must repay the debt in one to five years.

Credit Cards

If you, like 74 percent of Americans, carry a credit-card balance, find a card that charges the lowest interest and offers you the longest grace period before interest begins to accrue. If you pay off your credit-card bill every month, seek a card with the lowest annual fee. To find the card that suits you best, consult a personal finance magazine or search for one on www.cardweb.com.

Borrow Against
Your Real Estate

One source of relatively inexpensive credit may be your house or apartment. If you own equity in it, you can turn it into a piggy bank. This week, consider whether you should use it for that purpose.

When you borrow against the equity you have built up in your home, your choices include (1) home-equity loans, (2) second mortgages, and (3) refinancing. Of the three, the least costly usually are home-equity loans. They are essentially overdraft checking accounts that you can open at a bank or brokerage firm, using your home equity to secure the credit.

Home-equity loans spare you the hassle of securing a conventional second mortgage. After an independent appraiser values your house, you can usually borrow 70 percent to 80 percent of your equity in it. You must borrow at least $1,000 and are likely to pay an interest rate about one or two percentage points above the prime rate; but that is lower than the usual charge for second mortgages. In late September 2000, home-equity rates averaged 10.25 percent.

Many lenders may offer a below-market introductory interest rate for the first year, or even for three years, to win your business. The competition for it can be fierce. Major brokerage houses and even insurance companies are matching or beating the banks on home-equity rates. There is no penalty if you pay off your loan early. In addition, the interest on amounts up to $100,000 is fully tax-deductible, whereas the interest on consumer loans is not deductible.

Home-equity loans are sensible for major endeavors such as financing a child's education or an addition to the house. But because the funds are so accessible, beware of using a homeowner's equity account for risky investments. If you lose all your money, you could lose your home, too!

Here's another twist: If you're retired and own your home, you can take out a form of loan that allows you to collect monthly income from your property and still live in it. Look into a so-called *reverse mortgage,* sometimes known as a *home-equity conversion mortgage.* It lets you borrow against the equity in your fully (or nearly) paid-for house. You collect the loan proceeds in the form of monthly payments or a line of credit, or a combination of both. This goes on for as long as you live in the house, or for a shorter term if you wish. At the end of the term, you must pay off the loan and the interest, which may mean you will have to sell the house.

But elderly parents can sell their property to their grown children. The parents then can invest the proceeds from the sale in income-yielding securities *and* rent the house back from their children. In that way, the children get the tax benefits of owning and renting out their property—deductions for property taxes, mortgage interest, and depreciation.

The children must charge their parents a fair market value rent. However, they can *forgive* all or part of this rent by making it a tax-free gift. The limit for annual tax-free gifts is $10,000 from a child to one parent, or $20,000 if both parents are still alive.

Older homeowners also can consider a shared-appreciation type of reverse mortgage. It assures you of income for the rest of your life or until you move.

In one variation, you take out a loan against your house and pledge to give the lender a specific percentage of any future appreciation on the property. The more you pledge, the higher the monthly payments you collect. When you die, your estate may sell the house in order to pay off the debt. The lender then keeps the agreed-on share of any appreciation due, plus the interest on the outstanding balance. Anything that is left over goes to your heirs.

See If You Can Save
Big Bucks by Refinancing
Your Mortgage

Just like courtship and marriage, home buying is a two-part process: You have to find the right house, and then you have to find the right mortgage. The second hunt is nowhere near as much fun as the first, but it can be even more important. After all, you're signing up for a loan that will dominate your family's finances for as long as 30 years.

This week, investigate whether it pays for you to go through that tedious mortgage search again. Especially if you took out your mortgage in the 1980s, you may find that, by refinancing at today's rates, you can save hundreds of dollars a month—or raise thousands of dollars, perhaps to refurbish your house or to dispatch a child to college. In late September 2000, 30-year fixed-rate mortgages averaged 7.92 percent, and first-year rates on adjustable-rate mortgages averaged 7.27 percent. Those were nowhere near as low as a few years earlier (in 1997, fixed mortgage rates got down to 5.93 percent). But they were still much beneath the peaks of 1982, when mortgage rates scraped up against 16.91 percent.

In the days when you could get only a traditional, 30-year, fixed-rate mortgage, financial experts offered a simple rule: Refinancing made sense if your new loan's interest rate was at least two percentage points lower than the rate on your old mortgage. But, like most thumb rules, that one fell out of favor as the world of personal finance became more complex.

First, lenders came up with new kinds of mortgages. Today, you have a multitude of choices, including fixed mortgages with terms of 15, 20, or 30 years; five- and seven-year balloon loans; and more ARMs than a Hindu goddess.

Next, borrowers discovered that there were more reasons to refinance than just to nail a lower rate—for example, one could trade in the uncertainty of an adjustable-rate loan for the certainty of a fixed-rate loan.

Does refinancing make sense for you today? It depends on how you answer any of these questions:

1. *Will a new loan cut my monthly payments low enough to offset the cost of refinancing?* Your answer depends on the size of the rate reduction and how much longer you expect to live in your present home. Usually, you won't come out ahead unless you live there for three years or more. (See the Box on pages 137–138: "Will You Come Out Ahead?" for a more detailed explanation.)

2. *Will I come out ahead by swapping my adjustable rate mortgage (ARM) for a fixed-rate loan, even at a higher rate?* You can answer this question only with an educated guess. If you expect interest rates to rise still more in the future, now may be a good time to lock in a fixed rate that won't change over the life of the loan.

3. *Will swapping my current ARM for a new one give me better terms as well as a reduced rate?* You might get a lower limit on future rate adjustments, which would protect you from budget-busting raises in your monthly mortgage payments.

4. *Can I trade my 30-year mortgage for a shorter-term loan without straining my budget?* With a 15- or 20-year mortgage, you will pay off your loan much faster and save tens of thousands of dollars, but your monthly payments will be much higher.

5. *Will refinancing enable me to draw cash from my home, if I need it for some other purpose?* A home that you've owned for several years can provide money that you need for any major expense—renovations, medical bills, college tuition, and so on. You can tap it by refinancing with a bigger loan than you have now. (Other alternatives include home-equity loans and lines of credit, detailed in Week 20: Borrow Against Your Real Estate.)

If you answered *Yes* to any of those questions, you're a candidate for refinancing.

If you have a mortgage dating from the 1980s, when rates swooped to 16 percent, you have only one sensible choice: Refinance.

Cutting your rate from that level will save you tens of thousands of dollars over the life of your loan. And trimming only one percentage point from a 30-year, $100,000 mortgage saves you more than $25,000 in interest payments.

But homeowners still face a tough question: Will the savings be worth the hassle and expense of refinancing? Your answer depends not only on the size of your rate reduction but also on how much longer you expect to live in your home. Usually, you won't come out ahead unless you live there for at least three more years.

Whether you are refinancing or looking for your first mortgage, start by studying what local lenders are offering in newspaper ads. You also can get information on rates for mortgages offered by banks and other institutions in all 50 states and in 130 metropolitan areas from HSH Associates (1200 Route 23, Butler, NJ 07405; phone 1-800-873-2837, Web www.HSH.com). For $20, HSH will send you the latest reports and mortgage terms at institutions in your state, plus a Homebuyers Mortgage Kit that includes the booklet *How to Shop for Your Mortgage.*

You can get other pointers from a number of booklets distributed by the U.S. Consumer Information Center; for a free catalog, write to Consumer Information Catalog, P.O. Box 100, Pueblo, CO 81002, or call toll free 1-888-878-3256. You can also order publications online at www.pueblo.gsa.gov.

If you're refinancing, you may be able to negotiate with your current lender to waive some of the closing costs (as a way of keeping your business). If not, or if you're looking for a first-time mortgage, telephone a half dozen lenders and ask for their terms and rates. Make sure that the quotes are for loans that are identical in every respect.

The Internet can vastly expand your choices. You can contact mortgage lenders directly online—like www.e-loan. com or www.quickenmortgage.com. Then enter details of your finances and the amount you want to borrow, and the Web site will display the loans available. Many online brokerages will allow you to apply for the loan on the Net— you'll never have to deal with the lender in person. The papers are simply mailed to you for signing. That's the ultimate in electronic shopping service.

Whether you're refinancing or buying a home for the first time, you must find a mortgage that fits your budget and circumstances. Which of these three basic choices is best for you?

1. *Fixed-rate mortgage.* The interest rates do not change over the life of the mortgage—typically 15, 20, or 30 years. First-time buyers—or buyers who are stretching their budgets to trade up to bigger homes—tend to favor 30-year terms because they have the lowest monthly payments. They are also popular among buyers who expect to sell their homes within, say, seven years—the average length of time U.S. homeowners stay at one address.

With a 15- or 20-year loan, you pay a lower rate (an average of 0.34 percent lower for 15-year loans in September 2000). But your monthly payment is higher, and, compared with a 30-year loan, more of it represents principal payments. If you borrowed $100,000 for 30 years at 7 percent, you would pay $666 a month. With a 15-year loan at 6.5 percent, you would pay $871 a month, but you would own your home outright in only 15 years. Short-term loans are popular with people nearing retirement (they want to be debt-free before leaving the workforce) and with younger parents who face major expenses such as sending kids to college.

Alternatively, you can hammer down your interest costs with a 30-year, biweekly mortgage. As the name suggests, you make payments every two weeks. Result: You make the equivalent of 13 monthly payments a year, cutting 10 to 12 years off the life of a 30-year loan. Another choice: Simply add an extra amount to each payment. (Make sure, however, that your lender won't impose a prepayment penalty.)

Some financial advisers recommend a third alternative: Take a 30-year mortgage instead of a shorter-term loan, and invest the money you save as a result of the lower monthly payments. For this strategy to pay off, you must rigorously invest all your savings in mutual funds or other securities and they must return more after taxes than the after-tax cost of your mortgage.

2. *Adjustable-rate mortgages.* Most ARMs have 15- or 30-year terms, and their first-year interest rates are lower than those on fixed-rate mortgages. Even though an ARM's rate rises to approximately that of a fixed mortgage in the second year, the initial savings can make a significant difference, especially to someone who expects to sell the home in three to five years. ARMs are notably attractive to younger home buyers who expect to move on or trade up. It also pays to get an ARM if the lower monthly payments help you qualify for a loan on a house you truly desire.

Lenders usually adjust ARM rates annually, according to an index. The two most popular are the one-year Treasury securities index and the so-called 11th District cost-of-funds rate, based on a composite of interest rates that lenders are paying on deposits and their borrowing costs. The Treasury securities index moves more quickly, so it's the better bet when rates in general are declining.

An ideal adjustable-rate mortgage offers these features:

- Caps that limit interest-rate changes to no more than two percentage points a year and five to six points over the loan's life.
- An initial interest rate that is two to three percentage points below that of fixed-rate loans.
- No more than two points in loan fees (each point equals 1 percent of the amount borrowed).
- No cap on the monthly payment; otherwise, if interest rates rise high enough, the bank will add the unpaid interest to the principal, inflating the size of the mortgage.

If you can't decide between an ARM and a fixed loan, your best choice may be a convertible mortgage. It starts out with an adjustable rate that is lower than the rate on a fixed mortgage. But if interest rates drop in the future, you can convert to a fixed-rate mortgage between the second and fifth years of the loan for only a little more than the going rate for fixed loans at that time.

3. *Balloon mortgage.* This type of mortgage is structured like a 30-year mortgage, but the first-year interest is 0.25 to 0.75 of a percentage point less than that on a typical 30-year fixed-rate loan. However, you must pay off the principal—or refinance it—in three, five, or seven years. The deadline makes balloon loans popular with buyers who want the lowest available rate and expect to sell their homes before they must refinance. Often, a balloon loan will have a built-in refinancing option, offering whatever the going rate is at that time.

Another version is the two-step or balloon-reset mortgage. At the end of five or seven years, you have an option to pay off the loan or renew it for 25 or 30 years for slightly more than the prevailing rate on fixed mortgages.

To lower the rate on any kind of mortgage, you can pay your lender points (again, each point equals 1 percent of the amount you borrow). Paying two to three points for the lowest possible rate may make sense if you are planning to live in the home for three to five years. (Warning: Don't let the lender roll over the points into your mortgage. Over time, your interest payments on the points may cost you more than the points themselves.)

WILL YOU COME OUT AHEAD?

Homeowners usually should refinance their mortgages only if they'll save enough on monthly payments to come out ahead over the lifetime of their loans. (This assumes, of course, that they are not refinancing to draw money out of their home equity.) To calculate whether you will recoup the cost of refinancing, you must first have a reasonably clear idea of how much longer you will be living in your house. Then, use the worksheet at *Money* magazine's Web site (www.money.com), or take up a pencil and do the following calculation:

1. *Write down the monthly after-tax cost of your current mortgage* (divide the amount you deducted on last year's tax return by 12). Don't include insurance or real estate taxes in this calculation.
2. *Write down the monthly after-tax cost of the new loan.* Ask a lender for the amount of the monthly payment and multiply it by 1.00 minus your top marginal bracket. For example, if your top bracket is 28 percent, multiply the monthly payment by 0.72 (1.00 − 0.28).
3. *Subtract the after-tax monthly cost of your new mortgage from your old one to determine your savings.*
4. *Write down the closing costs.* (Your lender or lawyer can give you an estimate.) Typically, you'll pay 3 percent to 6 percent of the loan amount, plus any points (again, one point equals 1 percent of the loan amount) charged by the lender.
5. *Divide your closing costs by your monthly savings on your mortgage payment.* The result is the number of

months you must stay in your home to break even. For example, if your closing costs total $6,000 and your monthly saving is $150, you will need to keep your home for 40 months to break even (6,000 divided by 150 equals 40).

If the bottom line of your calculation is more months than you expect to live in your house, don't refinance. Otherwise, go ahead and swap your mortgage for a new one. After you pass the break-even point, your savings will be money in your pocket.

Start Investing
Profitably in Stocks

Are you one of the many people who say that they know they should be saving and investing more, but they just cannot scrape up enough money to do it? Here are eight principles that may help you surmount that problem.

1. Save regularly, almost religiously. Sadly, four out of ten working Americans have saved *nothing* for their retirement.

2. Try to save or invest at least 5 percent of your *pretax* income every year until you reach age 40. Increase that amount by one percentage point a year until you are age 45. Continue saving 10 percent a year. Ideally, you would raise your saving to 15 percent annually in years when you don't have college bills.

3. Pay yourself first, and save or invest that money. Every payday, write the *first* check out to yourself. That's the secret of saving.

4. Diversify your investments—for safety's sake. Start with mutual funds that invest in stocks. After you're comfortable with them, spread into some individual stocks and bonds.

5. Concentrate on stocks, which historically have returned an annual average of close to 11 percent a year in price appreciation and dividends. That's almost twice as much as corporate bonds have paid, and more than twice as much as the yield on U.S. Government bonds.

6. Invest the same amount of money every month or every payday. When markets decline—as they will from time to time—you can scoop up some bargains.

7. Take advantage of tax-saving plans offered by your employer, particularly if the employer contributes 50 cents or more for every dollar you invest. It's hard to find another way to make an instant 50 percent on your money. There is one exception: If the plan invests exclusively in the company's own stock and you are not confident about your employer's future, you might be wise to put your money elsewhere.

8. Invest in yourself. Learn new skills, perhaps at a junior college, so you can improve your earning power.

Now, having begun to apply the principles, you should proceed to invest.

With the stock market jumping or slumping in great gulps almost every trading day, you need to establish—or reaffirm—a *strategy* for investing, and then stick with it.

This week, determine what *your* financial goals are: To acquire a better home? To pay for the classiest education money can buy? To bankroll a secure retirement? Then calculate how much of your current income you can regularly invest, and what rate of return you would have to earn to meet your goals.

A reasonable return—price appreciation plus dividends—might be 8 percent. Don't expect to hit that target every year. You've done well if your *average* earnings over the years achieve that figure. You're in for the long term.

Figure out what percentage of your investment money you want to allocate to various categories—small-company stocks, large-company stocks, international mutual funds, tax-exempt bonds, real estate investment trusts, and the like. The way you allocate your assets among these broad categories will do much more to determine your success than will the individual stocks or bonds or funds that you choose. It's much more important to decide that you will invest, say, 70 percent of your available money in stocks than to decide that you'll load up on IBM or GE shares.

How you allocate your money hinges largely on three factors: (1) what purpose you ultimately want to use it for; (2) your age or stage in life; and (3) your own mentality. If you plan to use the money within the next seven years to pay your kids' college bills, don't put it into stocks (or mutual funds that invest in stocks). They can be awesome investments for the long term, but stocks are volatile and they can hammer you in the short run.

If you are fairly young, have strong career prospects, and have a long-term horizon for your investments, you can reasonably afford to pump a large proportion of your money into stocks. If you're older and in or nearing retirement, you're probably wise to put more into bonds and other secure (if slower growing) investments.

If you are over 50, you will probably want to put a large share of your spare cash into safe, income-producing assets. But you may well live a long life, and you will want and need some stocks to help carry you through all those years. Plan on having at least *some* money in stocks throughout your life.

A very important factor is your mentality or attitude. If you are a naturally conservative and risk-averse person, you're probably better off to stick with secure investments. Nobody can put a price on your ability to sleep soundly at night. On the other hand, if you are more willing to take reasonable risks, and you have faith that our country will do well and the economy will be healthy over the long term, you might shovel a large part of your free cash into stocks. Polonius had it right: "To thine own self be true."

What if you have only a small stake when you start investing? At least 150 mutual funds accept an initial investment of $100 or even less. Some have no minimum at all. For a description of nearly 4,000 funds, search your public library for CDA/Wiesenberger's *Investment Companies Yearbook*. Or visit www.morningstar.com on the Web.

Don't try to "time" the market. People who attempt to guess exactly when Wall Street will make a major swing are usually wrong. It cannot be repeated often enough: Investors who withdraw their money during tough times often miss out on the inevitable rallies.

A recent T. Rowe Price study examined the difference between a buy-and-hold investment philosophy and an in-and-out investment philosophy. Consider the 10 years between June 30, 1989, and June 30, 1999:

If you missed the best 90 days of growth in the market, you would have come out with a net loss. And even if you missed only the best 10 days, the decline in gains would be significant. Look at the chart below.

Value of $1,000 Invested at Start of Period
6/30/89 through 6/30/99

Stay invested for entire period	$5,590
Miss the 10 best days	$3,860
Miss the 20 best days	$1,900
Miss the 30 best days	$1,300
Miss the 90 best days	$ 780

Don't try to wring out every last nickel of profit. If you do, you may be tempted to try to buy in at the very top of the market cycle and sell out at the very bottom. Nobody—but nobody—is prescient enough to do that consistently. You're much better off to stick with your long-term strategy and continue investing the same amount of money month after month.

Remember: Stocks are the best investments for most people over the long term.

But the last two words in that sentence are crucial: *long term.*

Repeating our earlier warning: Don't put into stocks your 15-year-old's college fund or any other money that you'll really need over the next five years or so. J.P. Morgan said, famously, "The market will fluctuate." Let me add to that a bit and say: In this new era, stock markets will fluctuate *sharply*.

Don't panic when they do. If you're a long-term investor, you probably will be able to weather the periodic cracks in the market—and do very well.

I still think your best bet is "income averaging." Figure out what you can comfortably stash away, and then put a fixed amount into your various investments every month or with every paycheck. When markets go up, you can happily count your paper profits. When markets go down, you can figure that you're at a bargain sale. Last month, your regular investment could buy only, say, three shares of your favorite mutual fund. But this month, the same amount of investment money will buy you four shares!

Almost certainly, at some point in the future, the stock market will have a significant drop. What should you do with your stocks when Wall Street lays its next egg? There's a forceful argument that you should do *nothing*.

Many people go into a frenzy and dump stocks whenever the market swoons. That is a world-class blunder. Markets often make their sharpest gains after deep or lengthy slumps.

Even if you make a lucky guess and can tell, almost to the moment, when the market will start to take a tumble, you probably aren't lucky enough to spot when it's time to turn around and start *buying* again.

But under what circumstances should you sell? A strong reason for selling occurs if some stocks in your portfolio have spurted or slumped so much that they have thrown your asset allocation out of kilter. For example, technology stocks have jumped so high that you may have a larger proportion of tech shares in your portfolio than you had originally intended. It may be time to trim.

Whenever and whatever you do sell, it's much better to sell shares that you have held for a year plus one day or more; they qualify as capital gains, and the federal income tax on your profits will be no more than 20 percent. But any stock you hold for less than a year and a day will be taxed at ordinary income rates, up to 39.6 percent at the federal level *plus* state and local taxes.

When you sell only part of your holdings in a stock, aim to unload those shares for which you had paid the highest price, those with the highest so-called "basis." That will hold down your taxes.

Say you paid $90 a share for a stock and you sell it for $100 a share. Your taxable profit will be only $10. But if you paid $10 for a stock and then sold it at $100, your taxable profit will be a walloping $90.

If you absolutely *have* to sell a low-basis stock, try to offset the taxes by also selling off different stocks in which you have losses.

Look Into Investing in Bonds

The stock market seems so frothy and vulnerable that you may well be looking for other places to invest your money. One obvious haven to study up on this week is the good old bond market. To ensure you a fixed income over time, nothing compares with a well-constructed portfolio of bonds. As they say on Wall Street: Stocks help you to dine well, but bonds help you to sleep well.

With bonds, you have a vast variety of choices. Still, most individual investors should stick to bonds that have the top quality ratings: AAA or AA. U.S. Treasury securities, which are guaranteed by the federal government, are even safer than AAA corporate or municipal bonds ("munis"). Corporates and munis yield more than Treasuries because buyers take a chance, however slight, that the company or agency that issues the bond might fall into trouble and fail to pay its scheduled interest or principal. But the U.S. Government would have to collapse before Treasury securities plotz.

Some adventurous buyers with deep pockets and low blood pressure might consider lesser-quality issues. A bond rated BBB often yields one and a half to two percentage points more than one rated a royal blue AAA. Yields on junk bonds—those rated BB+ or lower by Standard & Poor's—are still richer because there are bigger risks in the junkyard. Interest payments could be deferred, or the bond's quality rating could be lowered further, depressing the price.

It's wise to spread your bond money over a range of maturities, from as short as two years to no longer than 10 or (at most) 15 years. You seldom earn much extra income for tying up your money any longer than 15 years.

When you buy a broad range of maturities, that's called "laddering" your maturities. It's a form of protection:

- If and when interest rates *rise,* the price of bonds will fall. But you will be in a position where some of your shorter-term bonds will be maturing fairly soon and paying off at full face value. You then can reinvest this money in lower-price, higher-income bonds.
- If and when interest rates *fall,* your 10-year and 15-year bonds will have locked in higher yields than the market offers. Thus, their price will go up, and you can sell them and reap some profits if you wish.

Why do bond prices fall when rates rise—and vice versa? Look at an example. If you buy a $10,000 bond paying 6 percent, you stand to collect annual interest of $600. But if, two years later, rates in the marketplace shoot up to, say, 12 percent, an investor buying a $10,000 bond would get annual interest of $1,200. If you wanted to sell your 6 percent bond, it would be worth only $5,000 or so. Reason: The buyer would need *two* of your nebbish old bonds to collect the current annual interest of $1,200.

Remember that bonds move perversely: When rates rise, bond prices fall. The other side of the coin is: When rates fall, bond prices rise.

Here's a reminder: The interest on Treasury securities is exempt from state and local taxes. Sorry, you do have to pay federal taxes on it. But interest from municipal bonds is totally tax-free. It is exempt from federal taxes *and* from state and local income taxes *if* the bonds you buy have been issued by an agency in the state where you live.

In one sense, municipal bonds have been big bargains lately, particularly in contrast to the 30-year U.S. Treasury bonds with which they are often compared.

Because of their richer after-tax interest rates, munis are considered to be good buys when they yield just 85 percent as much as Treasuries. Anything above that amount is pure gravy.

And how have munis been faring lately?

In mid-2000, high-rated munis were yielding, on average, a walloping 96 percent as much as Treasuries. You could buy a muni for virtually the same price as a Treasury bond. The yield on the muni would be totally tax-free but you would have to pay federal taxes on the Treasury's yield.

This would make a huge difference for people who (1) live in a high-tax state, and/or (2) live in New York City or some other municipality that imposes local income taxes, and/or (3) are in high tax brackets.

In late September 2000, municipal bonds with AAA ratings were yielding a plummy 5.5 percent, or even higher. You could buy insured AAA bonds issued by New York City agencies at 5.5 percent, and if you were a resident of Gotham, they would be triple-tax-free; if you lived in New York State, they would be double-tax-free.

You could buy similar AAA-rated muni bonds issued in Florida and yielding 5.4 percent. Or in Puerto Rico, AAA-rated and insured against default, at 5.4 percent. Or in California, AA rated, at 5.35 percent. Or in Pennsylvania, AAA-rated and insured, at 5.50 percent.

For updated yield and price listings, go to the Internet and visit www.investingbonds.com or www.lebenthal.com.

You can diversify, of course, by investing in a bond mutual fund. The risk—and potential reward—of a bond fund is that its price, or face value, rides up and down along with interest rates. When rates climb, the prices of fund shares decline. And when rates decline, the prices of bond shares rise.

You confront much the same risk/reward factor with an individual bond. The major difference is that, if you're patient, you'll eventually collect 100 cents on your dollar—when your individual bond matures or comes due, usually many years from now. But there's no guarantee that you will ever get back all that you put into a bond mutual fund. If interest rates keep going up and up for years, the face value of your bond fund will go down and down.

On the other hand, if rates decline in the future, the price of your bond fund shares will go up. Then you'll not only collect relatively high yields but, if you choose to sell, you'll realize a nifty capital gain.

Given the wide selection of tax-free bonds, what kind of bonds or bond funds should you buy? The answer depends on your financial situation and your personal psyche—notably, how much risk you are prepared to accept.

Say that you're relatively young—from your mid-20s to your late 40s—and you have strong career prospects; you have about $400,000 to $500,000 in liquid assets, and you can afford to take intelligent risks. "In that case," says Alexandra Lebenthal, CEO of the bond investment house that bears her family name, "I would probably recommend one of two things: either a municipal bond mutual fund or an individually managed bond account." (If you have $250,000 or more to invest, you can get an individual manager. He or she will extensively interview you and tailor a portfolio to your wants, needs, and goals.)

What about a couple, say, 55 years old, with a household net worth of about $800,000, who want to put money away for retirement? Says Lebenthal: "I'd look very carefully at laddering a portfolio of bonds so that if these people are planning to retire in about 10 years, they'll be building to a point where they'll have something coming due every year. We hope that they will be able to reinvest some or all of the money they collect."

Lebenthal would start to ladder with five-year bonds and then stretch out to longer maturities. The longer the maturity, the higher the yield. A five-year AAA-rated muni might yield about 4.5 percent, and a longer maturity would yield more.

And what sort of a bond portfolio would be wise for a retired couple, say, in their early 70s? Lebenthal says, "I'd recommend mostly long-term bonds to give these people the highest yield possible."

In addition, she suggests that this retired couple should buy zero-coupon bonds and give them to their grandchildren for their college education—up to the federal maximum of $10,000 a year in tax-free gifts to any person.

Why invest in zeroes? Because you can buy them at deep discount prices, and they mature exactly when you want them to pay off certain bills, such as college tuition. For example, for $28,261 you could buy a 5.60 percent zero-coupon tax-free municipal bond that will pay off a full $100,000 in the year 2026. Meanwhile, you would not be taxed on the interest as it builds up year by year, nor would you have to pay any tax on it when you (or your heir) collect it.

If you suffer losses on bonds, there is a strategy for recouping some of them. The strategy is tax swapping, and it works this way. Say you bought a 5.73 percent muni bond in late September 1999 at par (that is, 100 cents on the dollar). The price of that bond has, by late September 2000, declined to about 98, so you'd collect only 98 cents on the dollar if you sold out. Instead of just selling, you may, in essence, swap your bond for a different but very similar muni, also selling at 98. You then could take a welcome tax deduction for your losses.

The bottom line is that you haven't really lost anything, provided that you plan to hold your bond to maturity. Then, to repeat, you will collect every penny you originally paid for it. And, in the intervening years, you will collect interest on the bond—plus that tax deduction.

The IRS does not allow you to buy back the same bond that you sold, but you can buy something very similar. For example, you could sell a New York State Dormitory

Authority bond and buy a very similar New York State Mortgage Agency bond.

Although defaults are very rare, you probably should buy insurance against them—just in case. Muni bond insurance costs only ¹⁄₁₀th of 1 percent for an A-rated bond or better, but rises sharply to ⁶⁄₁₀ths of 1 percent for a lower quality Baa-rated bond.

Here's another tip: When interest rates drop, private companies and state and local government agencies often "call"—that is, buy back—their high-yielding bonds, and investors are obliged to sell them back. By contrast, 30-year U.S. Treasury bonds are totally "noncallable." So you can hold onto these bonds for a long time—usually, until they mature—without fear that the government will force you to sell out prematurely.

Pay Attention to Savings Bonds

When I was a little kid in Chicago, we used to buy "Defense Stamps" for a dime or a quarter at any neighborhood bank or candy store and paste them in a handy booklet. When it was filled, we had accumulated $18.75— serious money in those days—and we cashed in the booklet for a Defense Bond (later, after Pearl Harbor, renamed a War Bond). Then we were let in on the real miracle: That $18.75 bond, which went to finance the WWII effort, would grow in just ten years to be worth a whole $25!

So did Americans first learn of the wonders of compound interest and long-term growth, and so did masses of us get in the habit of investing—initially in bonds, later in stocks and mutual funds. Today, those patriotic War Bonds have become U.S. Savings Bonds, and 55 million Americans own them. But the surprising news is that those old-shoe Savings Bonds have suddenly become a rather sexy investment.

In 1998, the U.S. Treasury brought out the new Series I bonds (I stands for "inflation indexed"). They guarantee to pay a fixed rate of 3.6 percent *plus* an additional increment to compensate for inflation. In September 2000, I bonds paid 7.49 percent. That was the highest consumer savings rate in the country at the time—ahead of the average rate on interest-bearing checking accounts (0.81 percent), bank money market deposits (2.11 percent), six-month certificates of deposit (5.27 percent), one-year CDs (5.65 percent), and 30-month CDs (5.73 percent).

Both the I and the E bonds have some other attractions:

1. You pay no state or local taxes on the interest you collect from Savings Bonds.
2. You may well qualify to pay no federal income tax on the interest if you use it to fund college or vocational school tuition for your children, your grandchildren, your spouse, or yourself.
3. You don't pay any taxes on the interest until you collect it—any time from six months to 30 years from now, as you choose (although, a three-month interest penalty will apply to bonds cashed before five years).
4. The interest grows at compound rates until you collect it.
5. All Savings Bonds are guaranteed by the U.S. Treasury, meaning that the U.S. Government would have to default before you'd lose a penny.

Yes, there is a certain gamble to the I Bonds: If inflation goes *down*, that 7.49 percent rate might also decline a bit. So, if you want somewhat more stability, you may prefer the more familiar EE Bonds. They pay 90 percent of the yields of five-year Treasury securities; in late September 2000, that amounted to 5.73 percent.

It's worth emphasizing that with both the EEs and the Is you can save money for college *and* get some nice tax benefits, provided your income is below certain ceilings. Just buy savings bonds and hold them until it's time to pay those college fees. Then savings bonds offer three major advantages:

1. When you cash in the bonds and use the money to pay for tuition, books, and other qualifying educational expenses, you may never have to pay any federal, state, or local taxes on the interest.
2. Not only your child, but also you or your spouse, can attend any qualifying educational institution.
3. When you buy the bonds, you do not need to know who will eventually use the money for college expenses, as you do with some other college savings plans.

The single potential problem is that if you have a high income, at least $81,100 for couples filing jointly and $54,100 for singles, when you *cash in* the bond, you lose some or all of the tax-free benefit.

If your employer doesn't have a payroll withholding plan to buy Savings Bonds, you can get them over the counter at just about any bank or savings institution, in denominations from $50 to $10,000. You can even have your bank automatically withdraw a set amount from your checking or savings account every month, or every quarter, to buy the bonds. And you can buy them online (www.publicdebt.treas.gov) and charge them to your Mastercard or Visa.

So, Savings Bonds have gone on the Internet and become part of E-commerce. Now, if they'd only bring back those stamps!

Choose the Right
Investment Mix

There's no neat one-size-fits-all formula for dividing up your investments among stocks, bonds, and cash. The closest is the "classic" division recommended by some professionals: Put 55 percent of your investment money in stocks, 35 percent in bonds, and 10 percent in cash—that is, money market funds, Treasury bills, and other safe and liquid investments. *The Wall Street Journal* periodically surveys brokerages and financial services firms and publishes their latest recommended asset allocations. Usually, the variations are small and hew closely to the classic mix.

Your own proper allocation depends on a host of factors: your investment goals, how long before you must reach them, your willingness to take risks, your age, your tax bracket, your need for income from your investments—and more. Thus, a conservative investor accumulating money for retirement might want to put just 33 percent of his or her money in stocks—and only in the shares of large, stable companies or of mutual funds that invest in such firms. A more aggressive investor might be willing to stick 75 percent of his or her money in stocks and favor small, fast-growing companies that offer the best chance for large gains (as well as the greatest risk of losing money). A high-tax-bracket income investor might favor tax-exempt municipal bonds, and an income investor in a lower bracket (usually 28 percent or below) would end up with more money in his or her pocket in the form of taxable Treasury and corporate bonds.

Let's say that you fall in the middle of the risk spectrum: You're cautious with your money but willing to take some moderate risks for the sake of bigger gains than you could get from, say, risk-free, short-term Treasury bills, which yielded about 6 percent for six-month paper in September 2000. If you're either more conservative or more willing to take risk than this hypothetical investor, temper the following advice accordingly.

Just don't make either of two classic mistakes. One is putting all your money in high-risk stocks in hopes of scoring maximum gains; more likely, you'll wind up losing a bundle. The other is placing all your money in bonds for safety; if you do, your money may be eaten away by inflation—or by the rate-hiking actions of a hyperthyroid Federal Reserve.

Even conservative investors need *both* stocks and bonds. History shows that, over time, you probably can handle the risk of holding shares in large companies, such as those that make up the Standard & Poor's 500-stock index. An instructive study of various asset-allocation combinations from 1960 to 1993 was made for the New York City money management firm of Neuberger & Berman. It found that if you had put half of your money in five-year Treasury notes and the other half in S&P 500 stocks, you would have achieved 91 percent of the equity-market return with only 59.1 percent of its price volatility. The S&P 500 has earned a compound average annual return of 11 percent since 1926, but this 50–50 mix would have grown at a highly respectable 9.35 percent.

Of course, those are average returns over a 33-year period—1960 to 1993. During that time, the bond and stock markets rose and fell; stocks crashed in 1973 and stayed down until the unprecedented bull market of the 1980s and 1990s. Also, most of us don't have 33 years until we have to meet our investing goals. So, the advice here will be tailored to what most professionals regard as the right asset mix for money that a moderate investor sets aside for emergencies, the down payment on a first home, kids' college bills, and retirement.

Emergency Fund

This fund usually should equal three to six months' worth of living expenses, and you can't afford to take chances with it. If illness strikes or you lose your job, you must be able to tap your emergency fund immediately. With easy access and safety as your biggest concerns, you might put all your emergency fund in a bank savings account. Banks typically pay less than 2 percent or so on the money, but federal insurance will protect you against losing as much as $100,000 if the bank fails (a most unlikely event). You could earn about a half percentage point more without giving up the insurance by keeping your emergency fund in a bank's money market account. But these accounts usually require a minimum deposit and places limits on the frequency of check writing or withdrawals.

Keep your emergency cache in a money market mutual fund. It will invest in the short-term IOUs of federal, state, and local governments as well as those of corporations and banks. The funds, which are sponsored by mutual fund companies and brokerages, had seven-day compound yields of about 4.84 percent in late September 2000. Many funds offer limited check writing. For safety's sake—the funds are not insured—choose one that is backed by a large, well-established mutual fund group or brokerage firm. Such companies have shown in the past that they are willing to make up any losses suffered by their money market funds.

If you're still worried about safety, choose one of the U.S. Government money funds. These funds hold only Treasury bills or other government obligations, which are as safe as Uncle Sam. The safety comes at a price: The government-only funds yield about half a percentage point less than ordinary money market funds.

If you're in a high tax bracket, consider a tax-free money market fund that holds short-term municipal securities. The interest on them is free from federal taxes.

A Down Payment on a House

Again, this is money that you can't afford to lose. But you don't need to have instant access to it, so you can afford to lock it up in longer-term investments that pay higher returns than money market funds do. You might consider bank certificates of deposit (CDs), which are federally insured up to

$100,000; in late September 2000, five-year CDs paid an average of 6.03 percent.

Once you've accumulated $1,000 to $10,000 in your down-payment fund, you have other excellent options. You might put your money in U.S. Treasury bills or in two- or three-year Treasury notes. The minimum purchase amount is $1,000. You can buy bills, notes, and bonds from banks or directly from the Treasury. To learn more, visit Treasury Direct on the Web at www.publicdebt.treas.gov.

If buying your house is three to seven years away, you can put your money in Treasury bonds (minimum: $1,000) with maturities that fit your time horizon. You might also choose a conservative mix of stocks or stock funds, but you run the risk of a market collapse just as you're ready to buy your dream house.

College for Your Kids

Your first decision is whether to invest in the child's name, to save on taxes, or in your own name. Best advice: If your child stands an excellent chance of qualifying for need-based financial aid, invest the money in your name. As mentioned earlier, college aid formulas usually require a student to earmark 35 percent of his or her assets for college bills before qualifying for help; parents have to put up only 2.6 to 5.6 percent of their assets.

How you should invest the college fund depends mostly on how far away your child is from freshman year. Here are some recommendations.

1. *Until a child is, say, 10 years from college,* invest all your college savings in stocks or stock mutual funds.

If the market turns choppy or even crashes, you have plenty of time to make up any losses. For example, you might start out with an index fund that mimics the S&P 500, or a fund that's broadly diversified among large corporations. Then, as you accumulate more money, buy shares in additional funds. Ultimately, you should have your college savings divided among four or five different kinds of stock funds—for example, a large-company fund; a growth fund, which buys fast-rising shares; a small-stock fund; a value fund, which holds underpriced shares; and perhaps a fund that buys foreign stocks.

If putting all your money in stocks makes you edgy, then by all means invest a portion in bonds. Treasuries are probably a better buy than bond mutual funds; with Treasuries, you'll avoid having to pay annual management fees for an investment that you can easily make on your own. Be sure to keep your bonds' maturities reasonable; in late September 2000, holding bonds that matured in more than seven years didn't pay enough extra interest to compensate for the additional risk of big principal losses if interest rates suddenly shot up.

As an alternative, you can buy Series EE or Series I Savings Bonds; if your income is below certain limits, the interest will be tax-free as long as all proceeds are spent on your child's college tuition. (See Week 24: Pay Attention to Savings Bonds.)

2. *When a child is within seven or so years of college,* you need to turn more conservative. Gradually sell your aggressive small-stock fund holdings—perhaps liquidating 15 percent or so of your shares each year. Put the proceeds in more conservative total-return mutual funds, which invest for income as well as capital growth, and in short- to intermediate-term Treasury securities.

3. *As a child gets within three years of college,* start gradually cashing out of all your stock funds. At most, you want to have no more than 10 percent of your college savings in a conservative stock fund on the eve of the first college bill. Invest the rest in short-term bonds with maturities of one, two, and three years, and in money market funds.

4. *When college is less than a year away,* switch enough cash into a money market fund to take care of bills for your kid's freshman year. Invest the rest of your money in bank certificates of deposit or in Treasury notes with maturities timed to pay for the child's sophomore, junior, and senior year bills.

Retirement

In other weeks, you'll read about the advantages of tax-deferred retirement savings plans, such as IRAs and 401(k)s. Here, we'll recommend how you should divide your money among stocks, bonds, and mutual funds.

First, some advice about where you should do your stock investing and where you should keep your bonds. The "right" formula depends on your personal investment style:

1. *If you trade stocks often,* keep your shares in tax-deferred accounts, if you can, and your bonds in taxable accounts. Yes, you'll pay income tax on your bond interest (and capital gains if you trade your bonds for a profit). But your stock gains won't be subject to tax until you withdraw them after retirement.

2. *If you are a buy-and-hold investor*—you tend to hold stocks at least 18 months—then keep your shares in your taxable accounts and your bonds in your tax-deferred accounts. Taxes on your earnings from both types of investments will then be postponed—until you withdraw your bond interest and until you sell your stocks. Even then, you'll pay capital gains taxes on your stock profits at the lowest rate (20 percent).

Here are some fairly aggressive recommendations for how to allocate your retirement portfolio; again, the asset mix depends mostly on how far you are from leaving the workforce for good.

1. *With 20 years to retirement,* keep 80 percent of your investment money in stocks or stock mutual funds. Many investment pros recommend, for example, that you put 45 percent in large-company stocks, 20 percent in small-company stocks, and 15 percent in international stocks—or funds that hold such stocks. Put the remaining 20 percent in Treasuries and high-quality corporate bonds (or municipal bonds, if you're a high-tax-bracket investor holding them outside of a tax-deferred account).

2. *When you're within 10 years of retiring,* trim your stocks to 70 percent of your portfolio and boost your bonds to 30 percent.

3. *In your first 10 years of retirement,* reduce your stockholdings to 60 percent of the total and increase your bond holdings accordingly.

4. *When you've been retired for 20 years or so,* cut stocks to 50 percent of your holdings. Keep the other half in bonds.

As time passes, one asset class will outpace—or fall behind—another. Thus, every year you'll need to rebalance your portfolio, selling some holdings in the overvalued categories and transferring the proceeds to the underperforming ones. But you'll never outgrow your need for stocks. As we noted at the outset of this chapter, if you invest entirely in bonds, you stand to lose more to inflation than you'll gain from safety of principal. Besides, as the Neuberger & Berman study found, with a 50–50 mixture of stocks and bonds, you may well come out ahead on two counts. If history is any guide, you'll earn a very respectable return *and* enjoy a high degree of safety.

Find the Best Broker for You

F ew things have been changed more by the Internet than
the process of buying and selling stocks and bonds. Once
upon a time the world of investing was dominated by traditional high-price brokerage houses. The increasing power
and popularity of the Internet in the mid- to late 1990s has
given birth to online investing—and the transformation of an
entire industry.

Before the rise of online trading, brokerage firms were
divided between traditional brokerages, like Merrill Lynch,
and discounters like Charles Schwab. Traditional firms
charged premium commissions on trades; in return, the investor benefited from financial planning advice and sophisticated market research. Discounters cut commission costs by
stripping down information services and letting the investor
make trades on his or her own.

Then the Internet exploded, and everything changed.

By 1998—still only a year or two after the Internet became a household word—about one-sixth of all stock trades were placed through online services. According to Gomez Advisors, an Internet consulting firm in Lincoln, Massachusetts, 7.1 million online brokerage accounts were open for trading in 1998, up from 1.5 million in 1996. By 2001, the number of accounts is expected to hit 18 million.

The reason for this boom is clear—online trading is cheap. Online brokers charge flat rates for trades—Datek Online (www.datek.com) charges a flat $9.99 for up to 5,000 shares; Ameritrade (www.ameritrade.com) charges $8 per online trade, with no limit on shares; and E*Trade (www.etrade.com) charges fees as low as $4.95 per trade for its most active customers. With account minimums as low as $250, the online brokerages are throwing open the doors to buying and selling stocks.

Both the traditional firms and discounters have taken notice. The behemoth of brokerages, Merrill Lynch, was charging traditional customers as much as $300 per trade when it entered the online arena in 1999. Now you can trade through Merrill Lynch online (www.ml.com) at a flat $29.95 (up to 1,000 shares; 3 cents for each share over 1,000). Merrill Lynch still offers more expensive, personalized accounts for traditional customers. But the $29.95 fee matches the same per trade charge levied by its former brokerage rival, Charles Schwab, on its Internet trading service (www.charlesschwab.com). Former discounters now join traditional firms in touting market research as the justification for online trading fees that are higher than those of most of the original online brokerages.

Online brokerage services offer a great deal of freedom and accessibility. Experienced investors—those who follow the markets closely, know how to research and pick investments, and don't want expert second opinions—will be comfortable in the new online trading environment. But a traditional broker–client relationship may be more your style. How can you find a full-service broker who you can trust—*and* afford?

Particularly for small investors, choosing the right traditional broker isn't easy. Some firms don't want to bother with anyone whose account is less than $15,000. They probably won't turn you down flat, but they won't give you much attention, because you won't be generating large commissions. Some firms charge $40 a year to maintain an account, and $50 a year if a trade is not made at least once every 12 months. These charges apply whether the account involves stocks, bonds, or mutual funds. If your portfolio is in the low five figures, you're probably smart to stick with no-load funds and avoid wasting money on commissions.

In your search for a broker, there's sound reason to favor large national firms, which are generally more hospitable than smaller brokerages to modest investors. Reason: Big firms stand to make a bit of profit from the sheer volume of their small accounts. Look for major firms that offer special services, such as cut-rate commissions, along with research advice.

If you plan to invest mostly in companies located in your own area, you might do better with a well-established regional brokerage. Such firms' strength is in spotting small local companies that become home-run hitters when national firms catch on to them. But small brokerages also have a disadvantage: They are often less familiar with companies located far away. Therefore, if you have a fairly large account, you might divide it between two brokers—one national, the other regional. You'll get diversification and the benefit of two investing styles.

For the names of regional brokerages, consult Standard & Poor's *Security Dealers of North America*, available in most libraries. It lists firms by city and state, with their addresses and phone numbers.

Whether you choose a national firm or a regional one, your toughest task is selecting the broker who suits you best. Solicit recommendations from your accountant, your lawyer, or friends whose financial circumstances are similar to yours. Collect at least three suggested names. If referrals don't produce enough candidates, write, E-mail, or fax the branch managers of brokerage firms listed in the Yellow Pages, and ask for recommendations. Set forth your financial situation and investment goals to help the managers make suitable suggestions.

When you have assembled your list of candidates, do a little research on each person before your first meeting. Call your state securities administrator—the number is in your local phone book—and the National Association of Securities Dealers (NASD) at 1-800-289-9999. They can tell you whether your candidates are licensed in your state and whether they have been the subjects of any complaints or disciplinary actions. Ask your state agency for copies of the brokers' Central Registration Depository (CRD) files, which list any complaints or disciplinary actions. You can then toss out any bad apples early.

Find the Best Broker for You

Next, make appointments with your final candidates, and plan to spend roughly an hour with each. Essentially, you need to make sure that the broker aims to help you become a successful investor and not just turn a quick buck. Unfortunately, you may have to ask most of the questions. Not long ago, *Money* magazine surveyed brokers at 21 leading firms and discovered that two-fifths offered advice without asking about prospective customers' tax brackets. Nearly as many neglected to inquire about household income. Roughly a third failed to find out customers' tolerance for investment risk or their financial goals. All this is critical information that your broker must weigh when making investment recommendations that suit your needs. If your broker doesn't take account of your personal situation and goals, he or she will still earn commissions, but you'll wind up with a portfolio of unsuitable—and perhaps unprofitable—investments.

To keep this from happening, go to each meeting armed with the questions in this Week 26 unit. You might even draft a financial profile of yourself to get the discussion going. List your net worth, your current investments and their value, and your investment goals (growth, income, or a mixture of both). Most important: Explain to each candidate how much risk you think you can tolerate. Would you be unnerved if you lost 20 percent or more of your money in a market drop? Make sure each candidate knows the answer.

Then, ask your candidates the following four questions.

1. *How long have you been a broker?* Ideally, you want a highly experienced veteran who has been through good *and* bad markets. Avoid an eager newcomer who will learn his or her lessons with your money.

2. *Where do you get your information about investments?* Your candidate's number-one source will probably be research reports generated by various investment firms. The best brokers will go beyond those sources and do some research on their own, particularly if attractive small companies are in their own backyards. Such stocks can turn into extremely profitable investments if and when they are discovered by analysts and recommended to large institutional investors.

3. *In what areas have you experienced your greatest successes?* The answer will help you weed out brokers who specialize in investments that make you uncomfortable—for example, chancy high-fliers that expose investors to far more risk than you can stomach. On the other hand, if you're a growth investor, you don't want a broker who specializes in stodgy income or "value" stocks or bonds.

4. *What kinds of investments would you recommend for me?* If they sound unsuitable—too risky, say, or too stolid—and the broker's rationale for them isn't convincing, cross him or her off your list. Your ideal candidate's temperament and risk tolerance should be roughly in line with yours.

Don't be shy about asking a candidate for 12 months of performance records for three current clients (unnamed, of course) whose investing objectives—and willingness to take risks—are similar to yours. That will allow you to compare his or her clients' returns against the appropriate market index—for instance, the Standard & Poor's 500 for investors who favor the shares of large, well-established companies.

You might also ask the broker for the names of clients whom you can call for references. Phone at least two or three of them. You may uncover some unexpected blemishes, such as a tendency to overtrade. This misconduct produces high commissions for the broker but, generally, low returns for the client.

Basically, you want an ethical broker who will use his or her knowledge and experience to help you make your own decisions. You must stay up-to-date by regularly reading financial publications, poring over research reports from your brokerage house, and perhaps subscribing to an investment advisory service. You don't want a broker who will make decisions for you. Above all, you don't want to give him or her the authority to make trades that you haven't approved. Such discretionary authority can leave you vulnerable to overtrading, or "churning," which can be a prescription for financial disaster.

After you've selected a broker, keep your expectations in line with reality. Even the most ethical brokers are salespeople, and they can sell really hard. Thus, if your broker urges you to make an investment that causes you to feel uncomfortable, ask these four questions:

1. *What are the long-range earnings forecasts for the stock?* To find out, ask your broker for a research report on the company. When you read it, remember that analysts rarely rate a stock as a "sell" for fear that management will cut them off from key information; instead, they issue coded recommendations. For example, "hold" or "neutral" usually means sell. Similarly, "accumulate" may mean proceed with caution.

Fortunately, "buy" and "strong buy" mean just that—and it's a particularly desirable recommendation if the stock seems underpriced and the analyst makes a convincing case that the company is turning itself around.

2. *Why should I buy this stock now?* You don't want to bother with a company when its business cycle is about to turn down.

3. *How does this stock fit in with my overall strategy?* The answer may be self-evident but, if it isn't, insist that your broker explain his or her case for buying the stock. Make sure that it isn't simply the stock of the day—one that brokers get special commissions or incentives, like cushy vacation trips, for selling. Keep your guard up.

4. *What's your 12-month target price for the stock?* You'll often find this in the research report. If the stock hits the target, you don't necessarily want to sell. But you do want to conduct some research to determine whether you think the price is likely to continue climbing. You might also ask your broker to help you set a price at which you would be wise to sell and cut your losses. Both the target price and the selling price will help you gauge the risk and potential reward that your broker sees in the investment. Don't forget: If you invest in the stock and its price plummets, you will lose money, but your broker will still pocket a commission.

Every month, your brokerage will send you a statement of your account. The report will list all commissions you pay for investment. Watch those commissions closely. You may well be able to get much better deals, *particularly* now that the Internet has created so much competition for your brokerage business. Even if you fully trust your broker, watch out for trades that you didn't authorize. If you find one, it may be a mistake—or, far worse, one that your broker made without consulting you. If that's the case, complain in writing immediately to your broker and to his or her boss, the branch manager.

A final note: After you have been with a broker for six months, evaluate your account's performance. Then do it yearly. If you invest mostly in big stocks, compare your gains and losses with the S&P 500. If your portfolio's performance, before commissions, falls below the index, call your broker for an explanation. Perhaps you're invested too conservatively and should expect to lag the S&P, particularly in a bull market. Or perhaps you need to readjust your portfolio by dumping some losers and putting the proceeds into potential winners. But if your broker doesn't have a convincing explanation—or you're lagging the index because you followed his or her errant recommendations—don't hesitate to take your money and run—to another broker.

Begin Your Search for the Right Financial Planner

Even though at least 200,000 people claim to be financial planners—some experts estimate the total at 400,000!—a good planner can be exceedingly hard to find. A prime reason is that the federal government and the states don't rigorously regulate this fast-growing profession, so anyone can be a self-proclaimed financial planner. Some supposed planners are outright charlatans; others are disguised stockbrokers or insurance salespeople who figure that the title will help them win sales. Still others are honest and well-meaning but ill-trained or inexperienced. Nonetheless, excellent financial planners *can* be found, and this is the week to start your search in earnest.

First, you must decide what you need from a planner. If you only want advice on picking stocks or solving a tax problem, you most likely would do better to consult specialists in those subjects. But if you want expert help in putting your financial affairs in order and getting on the road to meeting your financial goals, you would be well advised to hire a financial planner.

The best planners for most people are generalists who have a thorough knowledge of subjects such as household money management, insurance, investing, taxes, retirement, and estate planning. Here's what you can expect a planner to do:

- Help you calculate your family's net worth, so that you know for sure where you stand financially.
- Assist you in drawing up a workable budget to ensure that you aren't living beyond your means and to free up money for saving and investing.
- Aid you in allocating your assets.
- Help you manage your IRAs, 401(k)s, and other tax-deferring plans, and confirm that you have a proper strategy for eventually withdrawing funds from them.
- Check that you are adequately insured against sickness, disability, and death and that you are properly protected against lawsuits and damage to your cars and house.
- Devise a strategy to hold down your taxes.
- Draw up a plan that will enable you to meet such long-range goals as sending your children to college and retiring comfortably.
- Review your will and help you prepare an estate plan for passing along your wealth.

All this advice will be part of a comprehensive plan that can cost from $500 to $10,000, depending on your net worth or income and on the planner you hire. The planner should be willing to work with other members of your financial team—for example, your lawyer and your accountant. Finally, the planner should offer guidance in putting your plan into effect and providing continuing advice. At the very least, he or she should review your finances once a year to make sure they're on track. Such checkups typically cost 30 percent to 50 percent of the planner's original bill.

There are three main types of planners:

1. *Fee-only planners.* For their advice, they charge either a flat fee or a percentage of a customer's assets. Fees can range from $75 to $200 an hour for advice on a specific issue—for example, an early-retirement offer. For a comprehensive plan, the fee can range from $1,500 to $10,000, or from 2 percent to 5 percent of a client's assets. Fee-only planners sell only advice, so they are usually more impartial than practitioners who also earn commissions for selling financial "products" (e.g., mutual funds) to their customers. Common sense suggests that disinterested advice is not necessarily competent advice.

2. *Fee-and-commission planners.* Their fees for creating a comprehensive plan are typically $1,000 to $2,000. They also collect commissions of 1 percent to 10 percent on any financial "products" they sell to customers as part of their plan's recommendations. Such planners' advice can be skewed in favor of products that pay them high commissions. Still, this category includes many first-rate practitioners, and no customer *has* to buy the investments that a planner recommends.

3. *Commission-only planners.* This group prepares plans for free and earns income solely from commissions on the "products" sold to clients. Generally, financial experts urge you to avoid commission-only planners because they may be tempted to steer you into high-cost financial products purely out of self-interest. Most consumer complaints about planners involve those who earn only commissions.

Your first task in finding a planner is to assemble a short list of likely candidates—no fewer than three. Most planners work independently, but some are on the staffs of accounting firms, brokerages, banks, and insurance and mutual funds companies. To find suitable candidates, ask your accountant, banker, or lawyer for a contact, or find out who does financial planning for friends with trusted judgment and with a financial situation similar to yours. These four institutions are highly regarded sources of help:

1. *The American College,* in Bryn Mawr, Pennsylvania, trains insurance agents and others to be financial planners. Graduates are awarded the designation of Chartered Financial Consultant, or ChFC. Phone: 1-800-392-6900.
2. *The American Institute of Certified Public Accountants,* in New York City, has many members who are also fee-only financial planners and have earned the title of Personal Financial Specialist. Phone: 1-800-862-4272.
3. *The Financial Planning Association,* in Denver, Atlanta, and Washington, DC. The FPA's members

include both fee-only and fee-and-commission planners. Phone: 1-800-322-4237.

4. *The National Association of Personal Financial Advisors (NAPFA),* in Buffalo Grove, Illinois, accepts as
   members fee-only planners. Phone: 1-800-366-2732.

Make appointments for face-to-face interviews with
each of the candidates on your list. These sessions are free,
and good planners welcome them as a way to ensure that
prospective clients will not misunderstand what a practitioner can do for them.

You must ask these key questions during your prelimi-
nary interviews.

- *What is your educational and professional background?* You want to know what degrees the candidate earned and what he or she did before becoming
  a financial planner. If the practitioner formerly spe-
  cialized in a particular financial product—insurance,
  for example—you might find that he or she is biased
  in favor of insurance-related solutions to financial
  problems, even if better answers are available.
- *What financial-planning designations have you
  earned?* Favor candidates who have qualified as
  Certified Financial Planners, Chartered Financial
  Consultants, or Personal Financial Specialists. These
  titles should appear on the business card you are
  given. They do not guarantee that the planner's
  judgment is sound, but they at least indicate that he
  or she took the time to learn the details of the profession and of personal finance. Make a phone call
  to confirm that the planner has registered with the

Securities and Exchange Commission as an investment adviser.

- *Are you a member of any professional financial-planning associations?* In addition to those mentioned above, the Certified Financial Planner Board of Standards, which licenses Certified Financial Planners (CFPs), requires them to sign ethical codes. Members who violate the rules are punished with anything from public censure to expulsion.
- *How long have you been offering financial-planning services?* The answer you want to hear is at least three years, the time now required before anyone can earn the CFP designation.
- *What continuing education do you pursue, to stay up-to-date on financial planning?* The candidate should at least do the minimum required to retain his or her CFP certification: 30 hours of seminars, classes, or home study every 2 years.
- *Who is your typical client?* Be sure the planner is well versed in working with people like you. Most planners are generalists, but some specialize in, say, retirement or small-business problems.
- *May I have references?* Insist on getting the names of at least three clients, and be sure to seek their opinions of the planner and his or her advice. Also ask the candidate for a copy of a plan he or she has prepared for a client like you (with the name deleted, of course). Study the plan to make sure its analysis of the client's finances, and its advice, make sense to you.
- *How much time will you spend with me, and who will work on my plan?* Be sure that you're interviewing

the person who will analyze your financial situation and make recommendations. Avoid planners who assign that work to a junior employee. You can expect a planner to spend three or more hours with you, gathering facts about your finances, discussing ideas, and explaining his or her recommendations.

- *Have you been cited by a professional or regulatory agency for disciplinary reasons?* Most likely, you won't get a straight answer from a dishonest planner, but you can call your state's securities administrator (the number is in your phone book), write to the SEC (Public Reference Department, 450 Fifth Street, NW, Washington, DC 20549), visit that agency on the Web (www.sec.gov), and contact the planners' professional associations.

- *How are you paid?* No professional planner will flinch at this question. Indeed, Certified Financial Planners (CFPs) are required to give you this information, in writing, at your initial meeting.

- *May I have a copy of your ADV?* Certified planners are required to give you **ADV, Part II,** a report that they file with regulators listing their experience, investment strategies, potential conflicts of interest, and methods of compensation. (This last item will tip you off to planners who claim that they are fee-only but also collect commissions—for example, on insurance products.) Insist that your candidate also give you **ADV, Part I,** which lists all disciplinary actions.

- *How much wealth can I reasonably expect to accumulate in five years?* Most investors do well if they consistently beat inflation by four or five percentage points a year. Thus, the answer to this question can expose a planner who is trying to entice you to sign on with him or her by inflating your expectations.

- *What can you do for me?* A sound planner will not only analyze your financial circumstances but will ask you key questions. How much risk are you willing to take? Are you more interested in maximizing investment gains or income? How do you feel about borrowing to invest? What are your financial targets? After the planner has a fix on you and your goals, he or she will begin to make recommendations—for example, advising you to direct your investments according to a strategy that meets your needs *and* your nerves.

- *After you make your recommendations, how often will I hear from you?* That depends mostly on you. If you fret every time the market dips, you want a planner who will do lots of hand-holding. If you're an experienced investor, you want someone who will call only when he or she has something important to tell you—for instance, that the star who managed your best-performing mutual fund has just quit. At the very least, meet with your planner once a year to see whether his or her plan still makes sense and is keeping you on track to meeting your financial goals.

The one-year checkup is also an excellent time to reevaluate your planner. Here are signs that the relationship is working: You've met such short-term goals as learning to live within your budget and to save regularly, and you're making progress toward reaching such long-term targets as sending your kids to college.

But if you're disappointed—and the fault clearly lies with your planner and not with you—maybe it's time to search for another financial adviser.

Give Your Mutual Funds a Regular Checkup

Mutual funds provide risk-reducing diversification and professional management, so they take most of the work out of investing—once you have chosen them. But you simply can't afford *not* to check them periodically to make sure that their managers' performance is up to your expectations.

It's time to give your fund—or funds—a checkup. Resolve to monitor your fund investments at the end of each calendar quarter, when newspapers such as *The Wall Street Journal* and *The New York Times* report on fund performances over the past three months. You probably won't have to perform more than a cursory examination until year's end, when newspapers and magazines publish annual records, along with such useful benchmarks as fund category averages and stock and bond market indexes. Then take the following steps:

Step 1

Make sure that each of your funds are performing well. If you have a bond fund, compare its 12-month average yield with that of its peers. If your fund owns only stocks, compare its total return—capital gains plus dividends—with that of similar funds and appropriate indexes. A money-management software program such as Quicken or Microsoft Money can help you in this chore. You'll find indexes in *The Wall Street Journal* and other major newspapers. The important indexes are: the S&P 500 for large-company growth stocks; the Russell 2000 for small-company stocks; the Morgan Stanley EAFE for diversified international stocks; and the Lehman Brothers aggregate bond index for taxable and tax-exempt bonds.

If your fund has lagged behind by a point or more in the past year, put it on a watch list and check its performance during the next four calendar quarters.

You might phone the fund company to find out what the problem is. Alternatively, read the latest reports on the fund in Morningstar Mutual Funds or the Value Line Mutual Fund Survey, available in large libraries or on the Web at www.morningstar.com and www.valueline.com, respectively. If you don't like what you learn—or if your fund continues to underperform by three percentage points or more over 12 to 18 months—replace it with a more promising one.

Other excellent reasons to kick a fund out of your portfolio include a change in investing style, which demands that you replace the fund with one that follows the original style so that your asset allocation will stay the same. For example, you might learn from the fund's annual or semiannual report that the manager of your small-company stock fund has been loading up on the shares of midsize or even large companies. The fund no longer has one of the key characteristics that attracted you, so you probably should sell it and reinvest your proceeds in a true large-company growth fund.

You might be considering dumping a fund if it has been taken over by a new manager who isn't matching his or her predecessor's record. Give the newcomer two years to prove his or her worth. With a bow to the roaring bull market of the 1990s, even a lagging fund probably has brought you profits on which you'll owe capital gains tax when you sell it. There is no point in generating a tax bill simply because you were overanxious—especially if the new guy merely needs time to learn the ropes and ultimately turns out to be a winner.

Step 2

Figure out your overall *total* return. After you calculate the return of each of your funds, use the numbers to determine your portfolio's total return. Multiply each fund's total return—that is, its price appreciation plus dividend payments over the last year—by the percentage of your portfolio that the fund represents, and add up the results. You can then compare your total return with benchmarks such as the S&P 500 and either earn bragging rights or, if you fell short, figure out what went wrong. Fix any problems you find. Financial necessities such as financing college for your kids or a comfortable retirement for yourself have definite starting dates and cannot be put on hold while you wait for fund weaklings to regain the strength that initially attracted you to them. However, don't act too hastily and run up unnecessary tax bills.

Step 3

Rebalance your asset allocation. One key to successful investing is to never change your asset allocation, no matter what is happening in the markets—unless, as explained below, your needs change. The carefully tuned asset allocation you had at the beginning of the year may have been thrown out of whack by what has been happening in the markets. Perhaps your stock funds have turned in double-digit performances, overweighting your portfolio with equities. If your allocation is seriously out of balance, you will have to sell shares of the overrepresented funds and transfer the proceeds to the underrepresented ones, to bring your portfolio back into balance. You'll owe tax on your gains from the shares you sell.

Step 4

Shift your investment mix as your needs change. As mentioned earlier, the investment strategy that suited you well in your 30s probably won't work for you as you approach retirement and have to put more emphasis on preserving your capital. In that case, you might reduce your holdings in growth-stock funds and shift more money to total-return or bond funds. But don't make the mistake of dumping *all* your stock funds. In retirement, you'll need the gains that you can get from equities to stay ahead of inflation.

Adjust your fund mix as you close in on specific spending goals. For example, when you are seven years or so away from a child's freshman year at college, gradually reduce your stock-fund holdings and increase the amounts you have in total-return mutual funds and short- to intermediate-term treasury securities. If stocks plunge, they may not recover before the first tuition bill arrives in your mailbox. You'll then have to sell fund shares when stock prices are depressed—something you obviously want to avoid, not only to prevent losses but also to maintain your self-esteem and record of success as an investor. For more on how to save for college wisely, read Week 25: Choose the Right Investment Mix.

The Rewards of Keeping Good Records

When you sell fund shares, you typically will be unloading shares that you bought at various times and various prices. Figuring the tax costs can then be a real headache, unless you're liquidating your entire position in a fund. (In that case, you add up what the shares cost you, subtract what you received for them, and pay capital gains tax on the difference.)

Fortunately, you can choose one of four methods to determine your cost, and use the method that saves you the most *money.* If you have not kept all your transaction statements, the Internal Revenue Service will require you to use the FIFO (first-in, first-out) method, which is usually the costliest. With FIFO, you sell shares in the order in which you bought them. You may be unloading shares that you purchased years ago. They typically cost you the least and will therefore produce the highest taxable gain.

A better alternative is to use the specific identification method; you tell the fund company to sell the shares that cost you the most. However, to avoid problems with the IRS, you must have retained all confirmation statements for your transactions, showing the date, number of shares, and amount invested. Once again we learn that, when it comes to investments and taxes, pack rats always save more money. You can sell the shares by phone, but you must follow up with a letter to the fund company (or your sales representative, if you're selling load-fund shares), stating specifically the shares that are being sold. *Get a written receipt of the sale.*

The IRS has approved two other ways to determine your cost. With the average-cost, *single*-category method, you figure the average price you paid for all your shares in a fund, including those you sold. You then use the average per-share cost in calculating your taxable gain.

With the average-cost, *double*-category method, you figure the average cost of shares you have held for less than a year, as well as the average cost of shares you have owned for more than a year. You then instruct the fund company or your broker, in writing, to sell the shares with the lowest average cost first. (If you don't, the IRS will assume you first sold shares that qualify for long-term capital gains treatment.)

Both average-cost methods have a downside. You'll have to continue using the method you adopted when you liquidate additional shares of the same fund, unless you get written permission from the IRS to use a different method.

Warning: Don't pay tax twice on your fund shares. This can easily happen if your fund company automatically reinvests your dividends and capital-gains distributions— and you forget that the tax on these annual payouts has already been paid.

To avoid double taxation when you're figuring your taxable gain, remember to add the cost of reinvested dividends and capital gains distributions to the amount you paid for your original shares.

Make Your Money Grow— Drop by Drop

You rarely get something for nothing, particularly in the investment world. But you can do precisely that with dividend reinvestment plans, affectionately known as DRIPs. They let you buy shares, sometimes at a discount price, without going through a broker and having to pay a commission. DRIPs have other attractive features, so spend some time this week examining them as potential investments.

Besides avoiding brokers' commissions, DRIPs and mutual fund reinvestment plans offer four advantages over investing whenever you are able to set aside enough money.

1. *Automatic savings.* With a DRIP, you don't receive cash dividends; they are immediately plowed into new shares of the company. As noted earlier, such regular saving—or in this case, investing—makes piling up assets almost painless. Also, by forcing you to reinvest your dividends, DRIPs give your portfolio

a powerful boost. Indeed, over the past 70 years or so, reinvested dividends have provided roughly one-third of the growth in the Standard & Poor's 500 stock index.

2. *Small, affordable investments.* Many companies let you buy your initial shares from them and require only $250 to $1,000 for your first purchase—and as little as $50 a transaction after that.

3. *Dollar-cost averaging.* With a DRIP, you automatically adopt this strategy, which requires you to invest a fixed dollar amount at regular intervals—say, monthly or quarterly—whether the market is rising, falling, or staying steady. Your dollars will buy fewer shares when prices are high and more when they are low (and are reducing your holdings' average cost). By sticking to this strategy, you'll be less tempted to bail out of the market when share prices dip—and are therefore better buys.

4. *Compounding.* You regularly invest every month or each quarter, so your investments can grow fast, due to compounding. Suppose, each month, you put $200 into stocks that return 10 percent a year—one point less than the average for the past seven decades. You'll accumulate $40,969 before taxes in 10 years and $82,894 in 15 years, which could be enough to pay a child's tuition and fees at a top public university. If you paid federal and state taxes at a 40 percent rate, those figures would be $32,776 and $58,164, respectively.

Roughly 1,600 companies now offer DRIPs to their shareholders. Among them are some of the best-known: Ameritech,

Conrail, Exxon, General Electric, Home Depot, Johnson & Johnson, McDonald's, Philip Morris, Sears, Walgreen, and Wal-Mart. Some companies, mostly banks and utilities, give you a 2 percent to 10 percent discount on the shares you buy.

Not all DRIPs are created equal. To help you distinguish the good plans from the bad, here's a primer on DRIPs.

Your broker can tell you which companies offer DRIPs. Or you can get a list by sending $39.95 to Standard & Poor's Direct Marketing Department, Directory of Dividend-Reinvestment Plans, 55 Water Street, New York, NY 10041. The directory is updated annually. You can also find lists on the Internet (try DRIP Central at www.dripcentral.com and click on "DRIP Resources," or Netstock Direct at www.netstockdirect.com).

When you have acquired at least one share of a company and have become a shareholder of record, call the firm's investor relations office and ask for a DRIP application form. (Warning: To qualify, your shares must be registered in your name—not held by your broker in street name.) Your dividends will then be automatically invested in new shares of stock. (The company will credit you with fractional shares if your dividends don't cover an even number of them.) You will owe income taxes on each dividend, just as if you had received cash. You can buy additional shares through the same plan, either regularly or whenever you have some extra money.

You can buy your initial shares through a broker—and pay a commission, of course—or directly from almost 500 of the companies that have DRIPs. Some companies will let you authorize them to have money withdrawn from your bank account at regular intervals to buy shares. With some DRIPs, you can even sell your shares by telephone (others require written instructions) or hold them in an Individual Retirement Account. Such features give you almost all the conveniences of investing in a mutual fund.

As DRIPs and direct-purchase plans have become popular, increasing numbers of companies have begun to charge fees. For example, Gillette imposes a $10 enrollment fee as well as a $5 charge for each cash investment, plus 8 cents for each share sold to investors. Reinvesting each quarterly dividend costs a Gillette stockholder a maximum of $1.25. Also, many companies sock you as much as $10 a transaction, plus 10 cents a share, when you sell stock acquired through DRIPs.

Some companies fill orders in 100-share round lots whenever it's convenient. Others fill them once a month, regardless of what's happening in the stock market. Thus, if you buy a stock that's quickly climbing in value, future dividends could be distributed after the shares have risen to a higher price than you would normally be willing to pay. The lesson here: Never buy a stock simply because the issuing company sponsors a DRIP.

Instead, buy the stock and sign up for the DRIP only in the following circumstances:

- *You like the stock and would buy it even if the company offered no DRIP.* The best candidates are blue chips with steadily growing earnings and excellent long-term prospects—stocks that you would be willing to buy at almost any price.
- *You plan to hold the stock for five years or longer.* Over shorter periods, you lose much of the compounding

effect of reinvesting dividends in additional shares. Also, a company with regularly rising dividends is a plus for DRIP investors. Eventually, after they've ridden out any market dips, they should make a substantial profit.

- *DRIPs' fees are low.* Some 50 percent of DRIPs charge fees. Favor those with no or very low fees. Otherwise, make sure the fees don't exceed what you would pay to an online broker to buy stock in the company (about $30 for up to 1,000 shares at Charles Schwab). (The Netstock website mentioned earlier will alert you to fees charged by DRIPs.)

For timely information about DRIPs, you might consult two monthly newsletters: *DRIP Investor,* edited by Charles Carlson, a chartered financial analyst ($99 a year; 1-800-233-5922), and *Moneypaper,* edited by Vita Nelson ($47.00 for the first year, $81 a year thereafter; 1-800-388-9993). Carlson has written a helpful book, *No-Load Stocks* (McGraw-Hill, $12.50); Nelson is the author of *Guide to Dividend Reinvestment Plans* (free with a subscription to Moneypaper, $12.00 on its own; 1-800-388-9993). Carlson also runs a website (www.dripinvestor.com) that provides stock recommendations.

Be sure to keep records of the prices at which you bought shares through reinvested dividends. And keep your old tax returns handy; they will have recorded the taxes you paid on dividends that were reinvested. Those dividends should be added to your original investment in the stock when you are determining your ultimate cost basis, which does much to reveal your taxable gain or loss.

PUT YOUR FUNDS ON
AUTOMATIC PILOT TOO

Your mutual fund profits can grow quickly, if you direct your fund sponsor to automatically reinvest your dividends and capital-gains distributions. Call your fund company for an application. Your dividends, as well as your year-end capital-gains distributions, will then be reinvested each quarter. (You do owe taxes on the dividends and capital-gains distributions; thus, you'll want to keep good records so that the taxes can be considered as part of your cost basis when you sell the fund shares. That way, you'll calculate your gain or loss on your actual tax basis, taking into account taxes you've already paid on dividends and distributions.)

Beware, however, of hidden fees on reinvestments. Funds sold by brokers—for example, Franklin and Smith Barney funds—often nick you for 4 percent of your reinvestment. Instead, you may prefer to take your dividends and capital-gains distributions in cash and reinvest them on your own—perhaps in equally good no-load funds.

Start to Fill Holes in Your Insurance, Beginning with Disability

This week, we begin a five-week series of steps that could be among the most important of your life. All involve buying insurance to guard yourself, your family, and your possessions against disasters that could wipe out your savings and other assets—or make your spouse and dependent children welfare clients.

It's easy to put off buying insurance. After all, who wants to endure an agent's jargon-laden sales pitch, let alone confront one's own mortality? Who expects to cause an auto accident that might wind up costing hundreds of thousands—perhaps millions—of dollars? Who wants to be told that he or she needs to buy more homeowners' insurance? If you've been procrastinating about checking up on your coverage and filling any holes, now is the time to confront your insurance needs.

Three basic recommendations apply to purchases of all types of coverage, but particularly to life insurance:

1. *Keep control of the buying decision.* Most people let insurance agents tell them what they need. This is especially the situation with life policies, which are the most confusing kind of insurance and, according to the all-too-true adage, are sold, not bought. To stay in control, you need to know the insurance basics, which are covered here.

2. *Buy policies only from reputable and financially strong companies.* You don't want an insurer that might collapse just before you (or your family) file a claim. Before buying any policy, check the company's financial strength with one or more of these well-known rating companies: A.M. Best (Phone: 1-908-439-2200, Web: www.ambest.com), Fitch (Phone: 1-312-368-3100, Web: www.dcrco.com), Moody's (Phone: 1-212-553-0300, Web: www.moodys.com), Standard & Poor's (1-212-438-2000, Web: www. standardpoor.com), and Weiss Ratings (Phone: 1-800-289-9222, Web: www.weissratings.com).

3. *Deal only with a trustworthy agent who has your interests at heart.* Avoid two kinds of life insurance salespeople: (1) those who push policies simply because they pay the highest commissions, and (2) those who urge you to buy policies for the wrong reasons—as an investment, say, rather than to replace lost assets or income, which is the only sound reason to buy insurance. If you don't already have an agent, ask people whose judgment you trust—your lawyer, your accountant, or

knowledgeable friends whose financial situations are similar to yours—to recommend someone. When you have collected a list of three to six agents, call or meet with each of them and ask the questions listed in Week 31.

When choosing a life insurance agent, be sure he or she is a chartered life underwriter (CLU) or a chartered financial consultant (ChFC). Both designations indicate that he or she has taken courses on insurance and agreed to abide by an ethics code that puts clients' interests ahead of personal gain. (For more advice on choosing a pro, see Week 27: Begin Your Search for the Right Financial Planner; many of the techniques for picking a financial planner also apply to insurance agents.)

Let's turn to the specifics of checking up on your present insurance coverage and filling any holes. Start with perhaps your most important policy, one that only 40 percent of working Americans have: disability insurance. It insures what's probably your biggest asset—your ability to earn money. An employed person's chances of being disabled by injury or illness are far higher than his or her risk of dying before retirement at 65. A 35-year-old stands a three-times-greater chance of being incapacitated than of dying. So, unless you have substantial income from investments, trust funds, or other sources, it makes sense to buy disability coverage, despite the painful annual cost—anywhere from a few hundred dollars to $2,500 or more, depending on your age, your job, the amount of income you want replaced, and special provisions in the policy you buy.

Financial experts recommend that you get enough disability coverage to replace 60 percent to 70 percent of your pretax earnings from your job. (Actually, you probably can't buy more than that, because insurers usually don't offer it. They don't want to discourage disabled clients from seeking jobs when they have recovered sufficiently to work.) That should be enough to maintain most of your spending power, especially when you buy a policy yourself. Reason: If you pay the premium, your benefits will be tax-free.

Before canvassing insurance agents for suitable policies, ask your benefits office at work whether you already have disability coverage. Two-thirds of U.S. employers do not offer it. Large companies usually do, but their coverage may fall short of the 60 percent (of salary) benchmark. (An employer-paid policy's benefits are taxable to you because your company paid the premiums.) If you have company coverage, subtract the policy's maximum annual payout from 60 percent of your yearly pretax earnings. The result is the gap you need to close with a policy of your own.

Don't count on Social Security to get you through. You won't get a nickel from Uncle Sam unless you have been disabled for five months, you are so physically or mentally incapacitated that you can't do *any* job, and your doctor certifies that your disability is expected to last for at least a year or will eventually kill you.

If you can't buy additional coverage through your employer, you'll have to obtain a policy from a life insurance agent. To keep premiums reasonable, seek a policy that has the following features:

- *Defines "disability" liberally.* Ideally, you want a policy that will pay benefits if your disability prevents you from performing all the duties of your regular job. But these policies are very costly. The least expensive ones pay benefits only if you can do no work of any kind. If you're a college-educated engineer, you don't want to be forced to take a job on a widget assembly line because your insurer has decided you can work and refuses to pay you benefits. Best compromise: Buy a policy that will pay you monthly checks for the first few years of a disability that keeps you from doing your regular job, and then continues paying them if you can't perform any job suitable to your education, training, and experience.

- *Starts benefits 90 days after you become disabled.* You can get shorter waiting periods for higher premiums. How long you can afford to wait depends on your savings (see Week 25: Choose the Right Investment Mix for advice on building an emergency fund) and on whether your employer offers sick-leave or short-term disability benefits. If you have them—or have planned wisely for emergencies—you might extend your policy's waiting period to, say, 180 days, and cut your premium by several hundred dollars.
- *Pays benefits until you reach 65.* Your benefits will then last until you are eligible for Medicare and can begin receiving Social Security payments. A shorter benefit period will reduce your premium but could leave you open to a devastating loss of income; a longer period may make the policy too costly.

Look for a policy that additionally provides residual benefits, which pay partial benefits if you can work part-time; annual cost-of-living adjustments, to protect you against inflation; a guaranteed-increase clause, which will let you buy additional coverage periodically without a medical exam; a noncancellation clause, so that your coverage can't be cut off or reduced as long as you pay the premiums on time; and guaranteed level premiums, which will prevent your insurer from raising them. Some companies also offer policies that, even after you become disabled, let you boost your benefits and ensure your eligibility to buy long-term-care insurance. (Warning: Some of these special provisions are becoming scarce, so you may have trouble finding an affordable policy that offers all of them.)

You may be tempted to buy the policy offered by the first insurance agent you consult. But, armed with a list of the policy provisions you want, you would be wise to seek quotes from three or more agents and take the best deal. You might also ask any professional organizations to which you belong whether they offer policies with cheaper rates than you can get on your own.

One final piece of advice: If you're planning to leave a corporate job and become self-employed, don't delay buying a disability policy until you've gone into business for yourself. You probably won't have any income to insure in your first months of self-employment, so no company will sell you a policy. Do yourself a favor. Buy your policy before you start blazing a trail of your own.

Calculate Your Life Insurance Needs

Life insurance is one of your biggest expenditures, but getting clear, expert, objective advice on choosing the right policy at the best price isn't easy. That's largely because most counsel comes from agents and brokers who collect commissions—often, very fat ones—for selling policies to you. If you don't buy, their kids can't belong to the country club.

It's easy to see why salespeople's pitches often emphasize "permanent" (cash value) over "temporary" (term) insurance. Cash value policies cost you—and pay the agents—much more than term policies.

It's also easy to see why affluent families are catnip for agents. If an agent can sell a $1 million second-to-die policy with a $20,000 annual premium, he or she can earn $10,000 in the first year and $1,000 each year thereafter.

Commissions on whole-life policies typically amount to 50 percent to 90 percent of the first year's premium, and

3 percent to 5 percent of that amount every year thereafter—as long as the premiums are paid. A $250,000 term policy with a $300 premium might pay the agent only $150 for several hours' work. On a $250,000 whole-life policy, the agent's reward would be at least $1,500 from a $3,000 premium.

Commission-based sales dominate the market because most people won't buy insurance without sales pressure. When an agent gets a call from a client who says he might just want to buy some more insurance, the agent immediately suspects that the prospect has just received a very bad report on a stress test.

High front-end commissions are needed because most sales efforts fail and because it takes time to explain the policy and shepherd the application through all the steps. Front-loaded commissions reward agents more for finding new customers than for keeping existing customers happy. So, even though you're entitled to "lifetime service," you may have trouble getting your phone calls returned.

When scouting for a policy, interview several agents by phone and then pick the one who appears to offer the best deal. You can increase your chances of getting a knowledgeable agent—one who places your interests first—if you ask a few questions:

- How long have you been selling insurance? (Most new life insurance agents don't last even five years before moving on to another occupation.)
- Are you a Chartered Life Underwriter, and if so, do you participate in the PACE continuing education program? (This represents a dedication to becoming and staying knowledgeable, though it's no guarantee.)

- Which companies get most of your business, and why? (An agent can represent hundreds of companies, but he or she usually has a few favorites.)
- Are you willing to disclose your compensation for selling the policy to me? (This may help you judge whether the agent sees himself or herself as a professional adviser or a salesperson. You can download a disclosure form at www.glenndaily.com.)
- What services do you provide after the sale? They may include: (1) an annual review of your policy's performance relative to your original expectations and to similar policies in the marketplace; (2) a copy of rating agencies' reports on the insurance company's financial strength; and (3) any suggestions for making more effective use of your policy as your needs change—for example, by investing more money in the policy as a nest egg for college tuition or retirement. You can get a sample service contract for your agent to fill out at www.glenndaily.com.

Get referrals from friends, accountants, or attorneys, but remember that agents often have cross-referral relationships with other professionals. You would be wise to verify the agent's qualifications yourself.

You also can consult one of the few fee-only insurance advisers, though they are hard to find. Some earn most of their income from fees paid by their clients, but they may also represent and receive commissions from insurance companies for selling policies. But there are fee-only consultants who get no compensation from agents or companies for policy sales; they work strictly on a fee basis.

Expect to pay $100 to $250 an hour. For a referral to fee-only advisers, visit www.glenndaily.com, www.peterkatt .com, or www.deathandtaxes.com.

To help you determine any potential conflicts of interest, ask the adviser to disclose the sources, nature, and amount of all his or her compensation when dealing with you. (You can get a form for this purpose from www.glenndaily.com.)

For a low-cost second opinion, consult one of the online services, such as America Online or Compuserve, or financial planning websites, such as the American Association of Individual Investors at www.AAII.com. The sites have forums on insurance where you can get opinions from other buyers and from agents.

The size and type of insurance you require hinge on what you want it to do for you. Don't make the mistake of expecting it to do too much. Insurance should be designed to maintain, not to raise, your family's standard of living.

To figure out how much coverage you should have, estimate your family's living expenses. Then determine where that money will come from if you should die. Include your Social Security survivors' benefits, savings, assets that can be sold, and your spouse's income.

The gap between the costs you expect and the income you can count on is what you need to cover with insurance. If you are a middle-income person with dependents, you are likely to need coverage in six figures.

It is not unusual for the amount to be shockingly high, especially if you want to maintain your spouse's standard of living for decades. Suppose you have two young children and a 35-year-old spouse, and you want to provide: $30,000 (after taxes) for living expenses for 60 years; $20,000 for each year of college for each child; $150,000 to pay off the mortgage; and $50,000 for miscellaneous expenses. You need $2,160,000 of capital—and even more, if you don't want to touch your principal. Total Social Security payments might be worth an equivalent lump sum of $600,000, and perhaps you have another $200,000 in spendable assets such as certificates of deposit or listed stocks. That still leaves $1,360,000 to be provided by life insurance.

You may decide to make your goals more modest or to buy less insurance than you "need." Perhaps you'll conclude that your spouse won't live to 95, or can get by on $25,000 a year, or can be counted on to earn at least $20,000 a year after tax. Remember that the chances are high that you won't die before reaching retirement, and every dollar you spend on reducing the risk of premature death is a dollar that can't be saved to reduce the more likely risk of outliving your money.

If you're buying insurance to help pay estate taxes at some future date, you'll need to get a projection of those taxes, and of asset values, from your lawyer, accountant, financial planner, or insurance agent. Again, you may decide not to buy all the insurance that you "need," after taking other goals into account.

There are two basic types of life insurance: term insurance and cash value insurance.

Term Insurance

This is pure protection. It builds no cash value that you can draw out in the future. The two most common varieties are:

1. *Annual renewable term.* You can renew this policy every year until you reach a certain maximum age, but the premiums you pay will typically rise every year.

2. *Level-premium term.* Premiums remain flat for five to 30 years, after which you can renew the policy at a higher premium for another multiyear period. You usually must provide evidence of insurability to qualify for favorable renewal rates.

Cash Value Insurance

Unlike term insurance, this combines protection with savings. After paying the agent's commission and other expenses, the insurance company puts the rest of your premium into an internal fund, where it earns interest. Its growth lets the company keep your premium level for life.

Cash value policies come in many flavors; we'll discuss the four that are most common.

1. *Traditional whole life.* This is the oldest type of insurance. Premiums are fixed and are based on conservative assumptions that interest rates will be quite low and mortality rates will be quite high in the future.

Each year, the company pays to its policyholders a dividend that reflects the difference between the company's actual and assumed experience. Among other choices, you may use dividends to reduce the premium or to buy more whole life insurance—called paid-up additions—at bargain prices. Many companies allow you to add term insurance and paid-up additions to a whole life policy; in effect, you design your own customized insurance plans. This increases the flexibility of whole life in two ways: (a) It lets you pay a lower premium, and (b) it lets you reduce the commissions the agent collects. The trade-off of the lower premium is that the death benefit will grow more slowly than it otherwise would.

2. *Universal life.* This flexible policy lets you change the premium and the death benefit every year, within limits. There is no fixed premium, but the policy will lapse if there isn't enough money in your account to pay the various charges for insurance and administration. If you drop the policy during the first 10 to 20 years, most companies hit you with a declining surrender charge based on the amount of premiums paid. These charges disappear after you've held the policy about 20 years.

One common myth is that a universal life policy lacks a guaranteed premium that will keep the policy in force for life. You can get the same guarantees that whole life provides if you pay a whole life premium each year. If you pay a lower premium, you take some risk that you'll have to pay a higher premium later, but you can avoid surprises by asking the company to give you a new projection of policy values every few years.

3. *Variable universal life.* This type of policy allows you to choose among a family of stock, bond, and other funds, with a fluctuating value.

4. *Second-to-die.* These policies insure two lives—usually, a husband and wife—and pay off at the second death.

The premiums are lower than for a policy covering a single life. Second-to-die policies are popular with affluent couples; they use them to help compensate for the estate taxes that their heirs eventually have to pay.

In general, you should buy a cash value policy only (1) after you have taken full advantage of tax-sheltered retirement plans such as 401(k)s and IRAs, and (2) if you're sure you'll keep the policy in force for at least 10 years. The tax-sheltered plans are better investments, and the high selling expenses of most cash value policies cause you to lose part of your investment if you drop out early.

Says Glenn Daily, a fee-only insurance adviser: "The problem with cash value policies is that you have to hold them a long time before they build up enough assets—that is, cash value—to begin to equal what you could get with other conservative investments. But many people just don't hold their policies for a long time. Less than half of cash value policies are held for at least ten years, and less than one quarter are held for 20 years. People lose far more money each year from ill-advised purchases of cash value policies than from the well-publicized insolvencies of some insurance companies."

On the other hand, if you actually hold a cash value policy for a long while, you stand to do better than with term insurance. Two significant advantages make cash value life insurance a competitive long-term investment:

1. Earnings grow tax-deferred within the policy, and they escape income tax entirely when you die. Your beneficiaries will not have to pay federal, state, or

local income tax on life insurance death benefits. (But they will have to pay estate taxes, unless you have the policy in an irrevocable trust, just as with any other asset.)

2. If you cash in the policy, your cost basis is the sum of the premiums, without any reduction for the value of the insurance protection you've received over the years.

Say that you pay $1,500 a year, for 20 years, into a universal life policy; then you turn it in and collect a cash value of $43,000. Your taxable gain is not $43,000 but only $13,000 (that is, $43,000 less the full $30,000 cash basis), even though some of your money was used to pay insurance costs. In effect, these costs become tax-deductible because they are not added back to your cash value when the taxable gain is computed.

Cash value insurance produces the greatest benefit when it is held until death, because the accumulated investment earnings are not taxed at all. In most cases, this tax break overcomes the high expenses, so your beneficiaries will get more money, on average, than if you had invested the money in municipal bonds or short-term bond funds.

What if you're shopping for a term policy? Consider these four factors.

1. *The guarantee period.* Unless the size of premiums is guaranteed, you need to weigh the risk that the company will raise its rates in the future, or that you'll have to pay higher premiums if you're no longer in the best of health.

Guarantee periods range from 1 to 20 years. State regulations have a big impact on guarantees. More and more states are increasing the amounts of money that insurance companies have to set aside to back their term insurance liabilities. This affects the cost of providing long-term guarantees and will increase the rates for new policies. If you need term insurance for more than five years and want to lock in a guaranteed rate, you might be wise to buy a policy now, before the rate goes up—possibly by 25 percent or more.

2. *Renewability.* Most term policies are renewable to at least age 69, but there are exceptions. Renewability simply means that you have the right to keep the policy in force; it doesn't guarantee that you'll be happy with the price, which rises with the years. Anyhow, try to get a policy that's renewable for as long as possible, unless a nonrenewable policy is available at a lower cost and you're sure your insurance needs won't extend beyond the short renewability period.

3. *Convertibility.* This gives you the right to convert from term to one or more of the company's cash value policies without evidence of insurability. Find out how long you have the option to convert. If you buy a level-premium term policy and aren't able to demonstrate good health after an initial term period ends, it may make sense to convert. The reason: The cash policy will be issued at standard rates, but term insurance rates will reflect the company's expectation that the remaining policyholders are in less-than-the-best health.

4. *The insurer's financial strength.* If history is a guide, you can expect death claims to be paid promptly and in full, even in the rare cases when regulators take over a company. If you wish to check the financial strength of an insurance company, call one or more of the rating agencies listed in Week 30: Start to Fill Holes in Your Insurance.

Give Your Medical Insurance a Thorough Checkup

If your employer provides you with group health insurance, congratulations! The coverage automatically gives you a cornerstone of sound family finance at far less cost than any medical policy you could buy on your own. This is true even if, lately, your company has required you to pay more for your coverage—through higher premiums and steeper deductibles (the amounts you pay out of your own pocket before your insurance kicks in). Be grateful that you're not among the 44 million Americans—half of them from households in which at least one member is employed—who aren't insured against medical costs.

You probably would prefer to have a so-called fee-for-service plan, also known as an indemnity plan. With this type of coverage, you choose your own doctor and hospital, and then the insurer reimburses you—or pays the health-care provider—for your expenses. But in recent years, as medical costs have shot up, employers and individuals have

turned to managed-care plans—primarily, health maintenance organizations (HMOs) and preferred-provider organizations (PPOs). Both are less expensive than traditional
insurance, but they usually restrict members' choice of doctors and hospitals.

In discussing the health coverage that most families
need, we'll first advise you of what to look for in a traditional fee-for-service policy (if you can afford one) and then
give you guidance on choosing a managed-care plan. Finally,
we'll offer some pointers on an ever-more-popular type of
insurance you might consider: long-term care.

Fee-for-Service

To make your medical coverage more affordable, you would
be wise to pay routine medical expenses yourself and insure
against only catastrophic costs that could wipe you out financially. Any policy should cover the full cost of basic hospital services and surgery, as well as most of your bills for
doctors' services and prescription drugs that are above the
deductible that you select. You can get such coverage with
an individual major medical policy. To find out which insurance companies in your state offer this type of policy, call
your state's insurance department, usually located in the
capital. (Blue Cross/Blue Shield and Mutual of Omaha offer
individual policies in most states.)

Expect to pay a steep price—typically, $2,600 or so a
year for an individual policy and $6,500 for a family policy—
plus annual deductibles of $100 to $5,000, depending on the
size of the premium. In your search for more affordable

coverage, you might ask professional, fraternal, alumni, or religious groups to which you belong whether they offer group health insurance to members. You may turn up a less expensive deal than is offered by any policy that you can buy on your own.

If you're obliged to buy an individual policy, take the highest available deductible and co-payment—the percentage of out-of-hospital medical costs beyond the deductible that you must pay from your own pocket (typically, 20 percent). Both should enable you to save enough on premiums to more than cover an occasional budget-bloating medical expense. But protect yourself by making sure that the policy sets a ceiling on out-of-pocket costs in any one year. The right amount depends on what you can afford; typically, policies carry ceilings of $2,500.

Also, ask for the highest possible limit on the total benefits you can collect in a lifetime. To be safe, you should have a limit of at least $1 million for each family member. (If you have a company-provided policy with a lower limit, consider shoring up your coverage by buying a second policy; Mutual of Omaha is one company that offers such supplemental coverage.) Be sure the policy is guaranteed-renewable, so that the insurer can't cancel your coverage as long as you pay the premiums, nor arbitrarily raise your rates merely because you have filed several costly claims. Rates can go up, however, as medical costs climb.

If you're turned down for insurance by private companies, ask your local Blue Cross/Blue Shield for the dates of its next open-enrollment period. During that period, the nonprofit insurer will take all applicants, regardless of health. Or, ask your state's insurance department if the state sponsors a high-risk pool. Be forewarned: Coverage in such a pool costs 50 percent more than regular policies.

If you're planning to leave your job and will have to buy your own insurance, call your employer's benefits department before you leave. Ask about extending your existing coverage for up to 18 months under the federal Consolidated Omnibus Reconciliation Act, better known as COBRA. You'll have to pay the total premium—including what your employer formerly paid on your behalf—plus a 2 percent administrative fee. But you'll have plenty of time to shop around for a less expensive policy. Even if you're switching jobs and your new employer offers group insurance, you might need to extend your old coverage under COBRA. For example, your new policy may have a waiting period before benefits take effect or before the policy covers a preexisting medical condition.

Managed Care

As mentioned above, there are two main types of managed-care plans: health maintenance organizations (HMOs) and preferred-provider organizations (PPOs). Actually, there are two types of HMOs: (1) the "pure" variety, which require members to use only doctors and hospitals that belong to the organization's network, and (2) "open" HMOs, which offer members the choice of using doctors or hospitals in the network or going to a health-care provider outside the network, usually at a higher cost. Meanwhile, PPOs work like traditional fee-for-service health plans, except that there is an option of paying lower deductibles and co-insurance by using the plan's own providers.

Increasingly, employers offer HMOs or PPOs as lower-cost alternatives to traditional indemnity insurance and share the cost of the premiums with their employees. But if you are self-employed or are not a member of a group plan, you'll have to pay the full fee yourself.

To lower their costs, health maintenance organizations stress preventive medicine, starting with free annual comprehensive exams. HMOs do whatever they can on an outpatient basis. They often reward their doctors with year-end bonuses and profit sharing if they succeed in holding their costs below a set amount, and the best way to do that is to keep members out of hospitals. This approach has led to some widely publicized abuses, but it also keeps members' costs down. Best advice: If you have any question about the care you receive at an HMO, get a second opinion—even if you must pay for it yourself. A contrary second opinion will bolster your appeal if the HMO continues to refuse to provide the care you think you need.

Managed-care plans vary widely in quality. Before signing up for one, ask friends or co-workers who belong to it how they rate the organization. If you know an independent doctor, seek his or her opinion of the standards maintained by the HMO or PPO. Phone the organization's administrative office and find out whether (1) the HMO or PPO is affiliated with well-regarded local hospitals; (2) most of its physicians are certified by specialty boards; and (3) the plan is accredited with the National Committee for Quality Assurance (for HMOs) or the American Accreditation Program (for PPOs). Both use strict measures of quality in deciding whether to certify a plan. Then, check up on the organization's financial soundness by phoning the state office that regulates managed care—usually the insurance department. (In California, it's the Department of Corporations.) The state office can also tell you whether there have been many complaints against an HMO or PPO you are considering.

Long-Term Care

Studies in the mid-1990s indicated that more than 40 percent of Americans over 65 will eventually enter nursing homes, and many other people will require paid help in their homes. Nursing home care typically costs well over $30,000 a year, and Medicare offers little help. It pays for 20 days in a skilled nursing facility and part of the cost for the next 80 days—but only after a hospital stay of three days or more. So, short of depleting your assets until you qualify for Medicaid (the government health program for the poor, which does cover nursing-home costs), what can you do?

More and more people are buying long-term-care insurance. These policies pay as much as $200 a day toward a range of benefits, including the cost of a nursing home, skilled nursing care there or in your own home, and custodial care at home, if you need help with such routine activities as dressing, eating, and walking.

The policies, however, are most affordable when you're in your 50s—and are therefore least likely to need them. For example, a 50-year-old person seeking $100 a day with a 20-day deductible for nursing-home care would pay a premium of about $364 annually; the same policy would cost a 65-year-old person about $980 and a 79-year-old person $3,907. Therefore, unless you're reasonably certain that you'll need long-term care—for example, you have a family history of strokes or other debilitating illnesses—this insurance can be a high-stakes gamble.

Two categories of people don't need to roll the dice:

1. Those with assets of under $100,000, aside from their home. Paying premiums will cut too deeply into their budgets, and if they enter nursing homes, the costs will quickly deplete their financial resources, enabling them to qualify for Medicaid. (Warning: Don't transfer assets to a spouse or someone else to meet Medicaid's stiff requirements without first consulting a lawyer; if you make a mistake, you could be heavily penalized.)
2. People with assets—not including their home—of half a million dollars or more. They can probably shoulder the cost of a nursing home or of care in their own home without going broke.

That leaves the vast middle group of Americans. If you're in it and you're interested in buying coverage, you would probably be wise to consider only policies that provide the following:

- A daily benefit that will adequately cover your costs; this could range all the way from $25 toward at-home care to $200 toward nursing-home care.
- Coverage of the full spectrum of nursing care—skilled, intermediate, and custodial—and an amount equal to at least half the nursing-home benefit for any home care you may need. (Home care can include physical therapy, help with medication, and preparation of food.)

- No requirement that you spend time in a hospital or a skilled nursing facility before benefits begin, whether for care in a regular nursing home or in your own home.
- Explicit coverage of organic nervous disorders, such as Alzheimer's disease and Parkinson's disease, as well as any preexisting medical conditions.
- A daily benefit that rises with inflation and continues for your lifetime.

You can reduce your premium by buying a policy that limits benefits to four years or so, but this may mean that you're merely postponing the day when you'll have depleted your assets until you are poor enough to qualify for Medicaid. On the other hand, 45 percent of nursing-home stays are for less than three months and just over 33 percent are for more than a year. Limiting the duration of benefits may therefore be a successful gamble—but it's still a gamble.

There are more sensible ways to cut a long-term-care policy's premium. You could agree to begin benefits 80 or 100 days after you've entered a nursing home or qualified for care in your own home.

Be sure your policy is guaranteed renewable, your premium won't rise, and your insurer is financially secure. (Check its soundness with the rating companies cited in Week 31: Calculate Your Life Insurance Needs.) If you take out a policy when you're in your 50s and can qualify for the lowest premiums, and you pay those premiums faithfully for many years, you don't want to lose your coverage just when you are most likely to need it.

Cut the Cost of
Car Insurance

After slipping for two years, auto insurance prices have begun speeding up again across the country, usually by 4 percent to 5 percent annually. The cost per car averages some $700 nationally, but in a particularly high-premium state like New Jersey, it averages $1,150 a year. Wherever you live, your premiums probably will continue to climb as a consequence of the rising cost of legal judgments, medical care, and car repairs. Take this week to determine how you can slow down your insurance costs without sacrificing any essential coverage.

Almost all 50 states make car owners buy insurance. But more and more drivers have let their policies lapse because of steep premiums—or, almost as bad, they have bought only the minimal amount their state requires. These pinchpenny drivers stand to lose all their assets if they're found to be responsible for an accident and wind up being assessed damages that can easily run into the hundreds of thousands—or even millions—of dollars. In fact, uninsured and underinsured motorists have become such a menace on the nation's highways that wise car owners insure against them.

The standard auto insurance policy contains six basic types of protection: (1) bodily injury, (2) property damage liability, (3) collision, (4) comprehensive, (5) medical, and (6) uninsured/underinsured motorist coverage. In the 14 no-fault states, personal injury protection is also available. Each coverage comes with its own price tag, which you can raise or lower according to how much protection you buy. Here are these coverages and some advice on how much to buy.

Bodily Injury and Property Damage Liability

Don't skimp on this coverage. If you or anybody driving your car with your permission causes an accident in which someone is injured or killed, this part of your policy may keep you out of the poorhouse. Liability protection pays for an attorney to defend you against lawsuits brought by the victims, court costs, and any judgment against you, up to the dollar limits set by the policy. A typical barebones policy—roughly what most states require—specifies limits of $25,000 of liability per person up to a total of $50,000 per accident, plus $10,000 for property damage. Nearly everyone should buy much more protection. The typical driver needs a policy that pays up to $100,000 per person and up to $300,000 for all injuries in any one accident. The policy should also cover up to $50,000 in property damage. This extra coverage will boost your liability premium by about 25 percent, but it's a smart expenditure. Indeed, if you have substantial assets or a high salary that could be seized to pay off a court judgment, you would be wise to raise your bodily-injury liability limit to $500,000 or more. Better yet, you might get $1 million to $5 million of protection at reasonable cost with an umbrella liability policy, which we describe in Week 34: Protect Your Possessions with Homeowners' Insurance.

Collision and Comprehensive Coverage

Here's where you can save money. If you choose to buy collision coverage, your insurer will pay for repairs to your car after a smashup if it was your fault or if you can't collect from the driver who caused the accident. Comprehensive coverage, which is also optional, protects you against other losses—for example, if your car is stolen or vandalized, is hit by falling objects, catches fire, or is damaged in a flood. (Comprehensive additionally covers loss of items installed in your car, such as a radio, but usually not anything you are transporting in it; such losses are covered by your homeowner or tenant policy, as long as your car was locked when the theft occurred.) If you decide to buy collision and comprehensive coverage, remember: Your insurer will not reimburse you for more than your car's current retail value. Consequently, you might be wise to buy both coverages only when your car is less than three years old. To keep premiums reasonable, take the largest deductible—the amount you must pay before the insurer starts reimbursing you—you can afford. Car owners typically accept deductibles of $250, but we recommend $500, which will knock 10 percent off your premium. If your car is more than five to seven years old or is worth less than $1,500, you might consider dropping your collision and comprehensive insurance altogether.

Medical Payments Coverage

This will pay the medical expenses—up to a specified limit—of anyone in your car who is injured in an accident, regardless of who caused it. Only no-fault states require medical coverage (see below), and many motorists elsewhere skip it because their medical insurance will usually pay their expenses resulting from an accident. But don't forget this: Your medical insurance usually covers only you and your dependents, including kids away at school. Thus, we recommend that you buy a small amount of coverage—say, $10,000 or so—for the sake of nonfamily members who may have no medical insurance and may be injured in an accident while riding in your car. Otherwise, injured passengers would have to sue to collect under your liability coverage—an ugly situation that you might want to avoid.

Uninsured/Underinsured Motorist Protection

Given the frightening numbers of people cruising our nation's roads with little or no insurance, you really need to buy this coverage. It pays for injuries to you or your passengers—and, sometimes, for repairs to your car—if you're involved in an accident with a hit-and-run driver or one who has no insurance or too little of it to pay your claim. (You can sue for damages, but keep in mind that drivers with little or no insurance usually don't have a load of assets, either.) Most states require you to have a minimal amount of uninsured motorist coverage, but we recommend that you buy as much protection against underinsured and uninsured motorists as you carry under your policy's personal and property liability section. You'll probably pay less than $100 a year, but it could be money well spent.

Personal-Injury Protection (PIP)

States with no fault laws—an insurance agent can tell you whether yours is one of them—often require car owners to buy personal-injury protection (PIP). With PIP, no matter where you are driving, if you are injured in an accident, your insurer will pay your medical expenses, regardless of who was at fault (hence the name, *no fault*). Usually, you can buy as much as $50,000 of PIP. But if you have adequate medical insurance, it's probably wise to buy only the legal minimum—typically, $10,000. And if your state doesn't require you to buy PIP, don't waste any money on it.

As explained earlier, you'll pay a separate price for each part of your policy; the total—the premium you pay to your insurer each year—will depend partly on the limits you set on each section. But far more important are risk factors you can't control: where you live, your age, and whether your family has young drivers. On the other hand, there are steps you can take to make sure you don't overpay for auto insurance. Here are the most important moves:

1. *Shop around.* Get a half dozen price quotes from agents who represent different companies. Don't be surprised if the prices vary widely. In January 1997, *Consumer Reports* found that a retired couple who owned a 1994 Chevrolet Caprice and had no record of accidents or traffic violations would pay anywhere from $816 to $1,489 for the same policy from different companies in suburban Florida. They would pay $449 to $782 in suburban New York, and $344 to $1,016 in suburban Chicago.

To get a benchmark price, call a local State Farm office; the company is the nation's largest insurer and, in many areas, is among the least expensive.

2. *Get the best combination of price and service.* When you've found a likely policy, check the company's rating for financial strength, following the explanation in Week 31: Calculate Your Life Insurance Needs. You don't want the insurer to collapse just when you need it. Then research the company's reputation for service by checking with your state's insurance department, usually located in the capital. Large states, including California, Illinois, and New York, publish annual lists of companies with the highest and lowest percentage of consumer complaints. Ask any insurance agents you contact whether the companies they represent will reward you with a discount for accident-free years. In addition, how heavily will they penalize you for accidents or for tickets for traffic offenses such as speeding?

3. *Skip unnecessary coverage.* Insurers usually will offer you rental-reimbursement coverage, which costs $15 to $25 a year and pays about $10 to $15 a day toward the cost of renting a car while yours is being repaired. It's often a waste of money, particularly if you have a second car. (On

the other hand, you might want a little-known rider, which at State Farm costs $15 to $40, depending on your age and location, and pays up to $400 for meals, lodging, and transportation while you are waiting for your car to be repaired.) Also, think twice before buying towing insurance (cost: $10 to $15 a year for a maximum benefit of $75 per incident), especially if you belong to an automobile club that provides the service.

4. *Choose your car carefully.* Cars that are easily damaged in accidents, popular with joyriders, or valuable sources of spare parts are the most expensive to insure in every state. As you might expect, luxury and racy sports cars are among the most frequently stolen; station wagons are less often targets for thieves. Compact cars generally suffer more damage than full-size cars—and you don't even have to guess who usually comes out unscathed from a collision with a sports utility vehicle (SUV). (According to *Consumer Reports,* sports and specialty cars have the highest collision losses. They are followed, in descending order, by two-door cars, four-door models, and station wagons and passenger vans.) Similarly, passengers in small cars involved in accidents are injured more often than those in large cars.

5. *Ask for all available discounts.* In many states, if your car has an alarm or other antitheft device, you can save 10 percent to 25 percent on your comprehensive premium. Safety features such as air bags and automatic seat belts make you eligible for discounts, too. People age 50 or older can often get discounts of 10 percent to 20 percent. Drivers with outstanding safety records also qualify for discounts. If you have a teenage driver in your family, which can double your insurance costs, you can reduce the extra price if he or she takes a driver's education course, gets good grades in school, or goes to college more than 100 miles from your home. Some insurers offer discounts if you take a driver-refresher course.

As you shop for the best policy, keep this rule in mind: Never risk more than you can afford to lose, but don't pay to insure what you can afford to risk.

Protect Your Possessions with Homeowners' Insurance

Whether you own or rent your home, you need to protect your worldly goods against loss from theft or damage from fire and other hazards. This is as true for renters as it is for homeowners. But, surprisingly, about 60 percent of renters don't buy policies, even though they cost only a few hundred dollars a year. For that premium, renters can protect their possessions against loss or damage, and themselves against liability—for example, if a visitor stumbles over a child's toy fire truck and breaks a leg.

Homeowners get protection for their houses. If you own your dwelling and have a mortgage, you probably already have insurance because most lenders require it. But do you have enough? And are you paying too much for it?

You probably shouldn't buy either of the two lowest-cost types of policies. They are:

1. *Basic coverage,* which protects against damage or loss from fire, lightning, windstorm, hail, explosion, riots, other people's vehicles or aircraft, smoke, vandalism, breakage of glass, theft, and volcanic eruption.
2. *Broad coverage,* which adds these perils to the ones listed above: falling objects; the weight of ice or snow; accidental discharge or overflow of water or steam systems; freezing or explosion of home appliances or of air-conditioning, heating, or hot water systems; and damage from short circuits or power surges.

Instead, consider buying special form (also known as *all-risks*) coverage, which protects your home against all perils not specifically excluded in the insurance contract. (Among the typical exclusions is damage from floods and earthquakes; for that protection, you need to buy separate policies at additional cost.)

How much coverage should you buy? The simple answer is: Whatever you would have to pay for rebuilding your house if a fire or other disaster leveled it. To be on the safe side, get guaranteed replacement cost coverage. Then, you'll be fully protected even if rebuilding your house costs more than the dollar limit—also called the face value—set by your policy. Unfortunately, guaranteed replacement cost policies aren't available everywhere or for all houses.

If you can't get it, buy a replacement cost policy, which covers the cost of replacing your home up to the policy's dollar limit. Most experts recommend that you insure your home for 100 percent of its estimated replacement value. Your insurance agent can help you determine reconstruction costs in your area, usually with the help of established formulas and tables. Taking local building costs into consideration, an insurance company will typically set your premium according to your home's square footage, adding in any expensive amenities like a Jacuzzi.

Your homeowners insurance also covers any outbuildings or other structures on your property, such as a detached garage or tool shed, usually for up to 10 percent of the policy's face value. If you own, say, a barn, and replacing it would cost more than 10 percent of your policy's face value, you must buy additional coverage.

Another extra policy you may need is worker's compensation, if you employ domestic help either full- or part-time. Some states require such coverage to be included in homeowner policies or liability policies (described below); California, for one, requires every homeowner who employs domestic help—even a part-time housecleaner—to buy a separate policy. Other states don't require coverage. To determine whether you need it, ask your insurance agent what your state requires and to what extent domestic workers are covered under the liability provisions of homeowner policies you are considering.

If disaster strikes, your policy will pay for far more costs than just replacing or repairing your home. For example, insurance will reimburse you for living expenses while your house is being repaired, within either a time limit or a dollar limit—perhaps 20 percent of your policy's face value. The policy will cover other costs, such as payment for removal of debris, protection for your belongings while your house is open to the elements, and new landscaping. (Warning: Some policies won't cover vandalism or malicious mischief if you've left your house vacant for 30 or more days before the damage was done. Also, policies generally don't cover damage from wear and tear, rust, mold, pollution, dry rot, insects, and the like.)

Whatever policy you buy, don't allow rising construction costs to push the dollar limit below 80 percent of what you would have to spend to rebuild your home. If your policy's face value is less than that, your insurer usually won't fully reimburse you for a partial loss. For example, if your policy's dollar limit equals 70 percent of your house's replacement cost and you suffer a $10,000 loss from a kitchen fire, the insurer typically will pay you only $7,000. Even if you're willing to absorb the extra out-of-pocket cost for the sake of a lower premium, don't make the mistake of insuring your house only to the value of your mortgage. That protects your lender, but jeopardizes your down payment and any appreciation in the house's value since you bought it.

To guard against construction price rises that could reduce your coverage to dangerous levels, you can buy an inflation-protection provision, known as an endorsement, for less than $30 or so a year. Better yet, because construction costs climb at different rates around the country, ask your insurer to automatically increase your coverage each year, to bring your policy into line with costs in your area. Every few years, check to be sure you don't have too much—or, worse, too little—coverage. You can ask your agent for help or hire a real estate appraiser for about $150. Also, if you put an addition on your house—for example, a family room—notify your insurance agent so that your coverage can be adequately increased.

Generally, homeowners' insurance will protect your personal property—including anything you take with you on a trip, or leave in your auto—up to a total equal to 50 percent of the coverage on your house. But you'll get back only the cash value of your property—not much, of course, if your furniture is several years old. Thus, it's smart to buy replacement-value coverage on your belongings, which will add about 10 percent to your premium.

No matter what personal property coverage you buy, you must be able to prove what belongings you had and what they were worth. That's an important reason to compile a personal inventory, including receipts and photos—perhaps even a videotape of your belongings—and keep it in a safe-deposit box, as recommended in Week 37: Make a List of All Your Possessions. Also, bear in mind that policies usually cover antiques, artworks, jewelry, and furs for no more than $1,000 to $2,500. So, get your valuables professionally appraised and insure them for their market value either with endorsements (also called *floaters*) to your homeowners' policy, or with separate policies. If you work at home, your homeowners' policy typically will cover no more than $2,500 worth of business equipment; for more protection than that, you must buy separate coverage.

Your premium will depend on where you live, the reconstruction cost of your home, and several factors you can't control. For example, the closer you are to a fire hydrant or a firehouse, the less you'll pay. Wood-frame houses are more expensive to insure than brick or masonry ones. You'll also pay more if you live in a high-crime area or one with above-average construction costs.

No matter where you live, you can cut your insurance costs. Shop around by getting price quotes from a half dozen agents. But don't sacrifice safety for savings: Make sure any insurer you're considering gets top marks from the rating services cited in Week 31: Calculate Your Life Insurance Needs.

Ask about special deals, which are offered by most companies. For instance, houses that are less than five years old qualify for premium discounts of as much as 20 percent. Installing dead-bolt locks and smoke detectors can gain you discounts of 2 percent to 5 percent, and putting in an elaborate fire and burglar alarm may cut your premium by 20 percent. Some companies award 10 percent discounts to retirees age 55 or older. The reasoning is that they spend more time at home than people with jobs. Many insurers offer 5 percent to 15 percent discounts if you buy both your homeowners' and automobile insurance from them. Some insurers offer 5 percent discounts to loyal customers who have had policies with them for three to five years, and 10 percent off for those with longer records. Raising your deductible—the amount of loss you pay for, before insurance kicks in—from $250 to $1,000 can knock 15 percent to 20 percent off your premium.

Don't be a cheapskate with one part of your policy: liability coverage. It protects you if you (or a family member) are sued for injuries on or off your property, and it pays the damages if you lose or settle the claim. Most policies provide $100,000 in liability insurance. You're wise to increase that to the typical maximum of $300,000, which will cost, annually, only about $10 to $20 extra. If your assets are greater than the maximum coverage available under your homeowners' insurance, you would be well advised to buy an excess liability policy, also known as an umbrella policy.

To qualify, your insurance company will probably require you to buy $300,000 or so of liability coverage under both your homeowners' and your auto policies, if you own a car. But then you can buy an umbrella policy that provides $1 million to $5 million of additional protection for only a few hundred dollars a year. Such a policy will cover you and your immediate family from claims for almost every kind of liability—injury, libel, slander, invasion of privacy, malicious prosecution—except those related to business activities.

Beat the Burglars

You don't have to spend a fortune or create a moated fortress to have a burglarproof home. Technology has made electronic alarm-and-security systems more available, accessible, and affordable than ever before.

The base price for a system is about $1,250, though you can easily invest considerably more. You'll also need to spend about $25 a month for a 24-hour monitoring service that dispatches the police or fire department if there are signs of a burglary, fire, or medical emergency at your home. But you often can get discounts of up to 10 percent on your property insurance if you put in a comprehensive security system.

Before you do that, however, call the police this week— for a free security checkup. Your local cops often will send police officers to inspect your property and show you where it is vulnerable. You can call the National Crime Prevention Council's fulfillment center at 1-800-627-2911, or visit its website at www.weprevent.org for inexpensive tips to improve your home's security. You can also contact the Insurance Information Institute for a brochure titled *Home Security Basics.* Send a self-addressed stamped envelope to Insurance Information Institute, Attn: FB, 110 William Street, New York, NY 10038, or visit the website at www.iii.org.

Your home's softest spot is the door. Most burglars gain entry by kicking in a door. Your primary line of defense is strong locks—not just on the front door, but on *all* doors. Some of the locks that get the highest ratings in *Consumer Reports* surveys are made by Kwikset and Medeco.

If burglars can't break your doors, they'll try the windows, so you need sturdy locks on them as well. But be wary of burglar bars. They offer more protection from thieves, but they can be disastrous in a fire. The bars make it harder for you to get out of the house and almost impossible for firefighters to get in.

For more protection than locks and a barking rottweiler provide, get a comprehensive alarm-and-security system. It will make your home two to three times less likely to be burglarized.

You have a considerable range of choices. There are wired and wireless, monitored and unmonitored, dealer-installed and install-it-yourself systems. You can buy a slice of off-the-shelf, do-it-yourself protection at Radio Shack, Home Depot, and similar stores. Or, you can automate your entire home, integrating heating, cooling, lighting, security, and telephones with a more thorough and sophisticated computer-controlled network, for a grand total of $10,000.

A basic security system usually has: a control panel where you key in your pass code when you leave and enter; one to three motion detectors; one to three alarms; and devices on windows and doors that alert a central monitoring station if they're tampered with. You can buy all of this paraphernalia at a home-supply, hardware, discount, or consumer electronics store. But unless you're a do-it-yourself genius, you're much more secure investing in professional installation.

You should shop as warily for a security system as you would for a used car. When choosing an alarm company, be picky and ask questions. Consult friends and neighbors for advice. Ask the company for references. Check the Better Business Bureau for complaints.

Call in at least three companies for consultations and estimates. Brinks Home Security and ADT Security Services, for example, install similar standard systems. They include a motion sensor and indoor siren, among many other things. You get a keypad; you punch in a simple code to arm the system when you leave the house, and to disarm it when you return.

You should receive 24-hour monitoring from a central station; the people on duty there will call your local police or fire department if the alarm is triggered. They may first phone your home to see whether the alarm was set off by mistake. Ask whether your monitoring system is listed with Underwriters Laboratories (UL), which is a sign of quality.

Before you buy a security system, check out the person who puts it in; alarms are only as reliable as the people who install them. Get at least three competitive bids. Ask for and call references from several recent customers. Call the Better Business Bureau or your state or local consumer protection agency to see whether there have been any complaints against the installers you are considering.

Thousands of installers are members of either the National Burglar and Fire Alarm Association (NBFAA) or the Central Station Alarm Association. Both are in Bethesda, Maryland. The NBFAA (phone: 1-301-585-1855; Web: www .alarm.org) will put you in touch with your state chapter, which will give you a list of members in your city and will send you a free brochure titled *Safe and Sound: Your Guide to Home Security,* that will help you evaluate security systems.

Let's say you're buying a home security system to protect your property against burglary and fire. For a large home, or a house that has a lot of windows and doors or a cache of valuables, you will want something beyond the basic system. If you begin thinking about adding infrared-beam sensors, smoke sensors, floor-pad sensors, panic switches to automatically trip an alarm, glass-breakage detectors, or strobe lights, contact a professional installer who can help you decide what equipment you actually need.

If you choose a monitored system, learn who is going to monitor it. It may not be the company that sells you the basic alarm-and-security system. Many companies subcontract with a monitoring firm to handle calls, and that firm may not even be in your state.

Find out what the monitor response time is; it should be within two minutes. (A monitoring company uses 911 just like everyone else, and has no extra clout to get police or firefighters dispatched.) Ask whether it has backup in case of a power loss and whether it charges for false alarms.

You'll know that your monitoring company is secure if it has an Underwriters Laboratory rating; but lack of that rating doesn't mean it's a poor monitoring station. Companies that sell systems with 24-hour monitoring services nationwide include ADT, of Parsippany, New Jersey (1-800-238-7870), and Honeywell Protection Services of Minneapolis, with offices nationwide (1-800-328-5111).

A self-installed system can also be monitored. We Monitor America (1-800-221-9362), a UL-listed central station, will monitor your system for $15 to $20 a month, provided that a dialing mechanism can be plugged into the system.

For people building a new home, a security system can be just one part of what is called home automation—the integration of lighting, security, heating and cooling, telephone, and TV audio. With this technology, for example, when your alarm goes off at 6:00 A.M., the shades in your bedroom would slowly begin to go up; your shower would turn on, warming up to a predetermined temperature; the heat would be coming up; the coffee would begin perking; and lights would turn on in the rooms you would be most likely to enter. In the evening, you could tell as each child comes home because each would have a separate security code; motion and heat-sensor monitors could tell you which rooms in the house are occupied.

For a brochure about home automation and a list of dealers in your area, contact the Home Automation & Networking Association, 1444 I Street, NW, Suite 700, Washington, DC 20005; phone: 1-202-712-9050; Web: www .homeautomation.org. Among the reliable companies with home automation systems are: Honeywell (1-800-328-5111), Smart House (1-919-844-9025), and ADT (1-800-238-4636).

Now, a few words about safes. To protect gems, documents, and other valuables, bank safe deposit boxes are better than home safes. After all, the bank can invest more in security than you can. A safe can run from $900 into the thousands, but, unfortunately, many of the safes you'll see in office supply stores or hardware shops don't offer solid protection.

If you're thinking of buying a wall safe, think again. Most thieves can hack into the wall, carry your safe away, then pound on it with a sledgehammer until it opens. Your safe will be more secure if you install it in a concrete basement floor, but that requires cutting a hole in solid concrete. Once you've gone to that trouble, you're not likely to want to dig it out when you move, so consider how long you plan to be in your home.

A free-standing safe is a smart choice only if it is so large and heavy that two people can't lift it. In fact, the thicker the safe's doors and walls are, the better.

Underwriters Laboratories rates safes on their resistance to fire, as well as their resistance to tampering by someone using typical burglars' tools. A "TL" rating means the safe resisted attacks from hand tools, and "TRTL" means the safe also managed to repel attempts at opening it with a torch. The number following the letters—usually 15, 30, or 60—indicates the number of minutes the safe withstood constant attack.

For fire protection, the rankings begin with a number. If a safe is rated 350-2, the temperature in the interior of the safe will not exceed 350 degrees for two hours during a fire. According to UL, class 350 equipment protects paper documents, class 150 protects magnetic tape and film, and class 125 protects floppy disks.

Bar That Car Thief

A car is stolen every 20 seconds in the United States—and the next one might be yours. This week, buy and install security devices that will discourage thieves for years to come. True, professional car snatchers are so fast and experienced that police, insurance underwriters, and even manufacturers of antitheft devices say they're hard to thwart. But although alarms and other preventive devices are not foolproof, the right ones can save you anguish and expense—and at least put off the amateurs and casual joyriders.

Even if nobody ever tries to steal your car, you will get a 5 percent to 15 percent discount on your auto insurance for using an anti-theft device. Call the National Insurance Consumer Helpline, at 1-800-942-4242, for information on which security measures may entitle you to an insurance discount.

Antitheft devices now are so varied and sophisticated that you can outfit your car to do just about everything but roll over and play dead when it is attacked. You can buy many of these gadgets at stores that sell automotive accessories. But you're probably wiser to spend more and enlist a dealer to install a comprehensive alarm-and-security system. The dealers are far from perfect in installing these complex systems, but they'll probably do a much better job than you—unless you're a well-trained amateur mechanic.

The most expensive type of system sets off a siren at a variety of intrusions—for example, if someone bangs a window or jolts the car—and also has a device that disables the starter, ignition, or fuel system so that a thief can't drive.

Consumer Reports, in its latest survey of dealer-installed security sytems, gave excellent marks to Intelliguard products from Clifford Electronics (Phone: 1-800-753-0600; www.clifford.com) and the Python/Viper series of systems from Directed Electronics, Inc. (Phone: 1-800-283-1344; www.dei.com). Prices vary widely, depending on the bells and whistles you may add, but most are under $1,000. You can also save by buying only a device that prevents a thief from starting the car, like the Safestop Starter Disable from Harrison Electronic Systems (Phone: 1-800-422-5050; www .harrisonelectronics.com). Safestop Starter Disable incapacitates the starter each time the ignition is turned off. Your car cannot be started until a hidden pressure switch is touched.

If thieves want your wheels and tires, you can complicate their task by installing locking lugs. A set of four plus the special wrench needed to unlock them costs $12 to $45.

The most advanced type of protection is the LoJack satellite vehicle-tracking system, based on a small device that emits silent signals from a secret site in your car (neither you nor your dealer knows where it is). If your auto is stolen, just phone the local police. Police cars equipped with special receivers can track down your car and the thief. Many police departments use this product to follow their own fleets. Costs begin around $600.

Make a List of All
Your Possessions

To keep a burglary, fire, or other disaster from devastating your assets, make a thorough inventory of everything you have in your home this week so that you can document the value of any possession you lose. Your insurance company can give you an inventory form, or you can get a free brochure, "Taking Inventory," by calling the National Insurance Consumer Hotline (1-800-942-4242).

Go through every room; open drawers and cupboards, and carefully list anything of value. Don't forget to examine everything in your attic, basement, and garage. And don't overlook things that you are so used to seeing that they fade into the background—carpets, curtains, linens, and the like.

Describe every item in detail. Record any identifying information, such as appliance serial numbers and credit-card account numbers. If you ever make an insurance claim, it helps to include the age, brand name, size, model number, and other relevant details of just about any valuable object. For tableware, note the manufacturer, pattern, and number of place settings. Also, record the date when you bought an item, the amount that you paid, and how much it would cost to replace it. And of course, keep all sales receipts.

You might also photograph the contents of your home, preferably with self-developing film so that no stranger will see it at the processing lab. In addition, photograph each wall with all cabinet and closet doors open.

Better yet, videotape your possessions, zooming in on high-value items such as antiques. A shot inside the closet doors, accompanied by your verbal description, will spare you from having to write down the entire contents. Some independent claim services and camera stores will provide, for a fee, a video inventory of your home, although you may prefer, for privacy's sake, to do it yourself. Before you hire anyone, check his or her reputation with the Better Business Bureau and the local police.

In addition, get appraisals of art, antiques, jewelry, and other valuables, and—as suggested above—store the appraisals in your safe-deposit box. You can find appraisers through the American Society of Appraisers, 535 Herndon Parkway, Herndon, VA 22070; phone: 1-800-272-8258.

Your household inventory, backed up by photographs or a videotape, will help take some of the sting out of any loss. Your records will first let you collect as much as you deserve from your insurance company. Then, any unreimbursed losses that exceed 10 percent of your adjusted gross income, plus $100 per incident, can be written off on your tax return. Unfortunately, for tax purposes, you can figure your loss only on an item's current market value—not the amount it originally cost. Still, without an inventory, you could wind up with nothing.

Guard Your Family Against Natural Disasters

Firestorms in New Mexico and Idaho. Tornadoes in Utah and Oklahoma. Hurricanes in Florida, Georgia, and the Carolinas. Earthquakes in California and Alaska. Volcanic eruptions in Washington State. Torrential rains in Missouri and New Jersey. Floods in North Dakota and Louisiana. Tsunamis in Hawaii.

Natural disasters can devastate your possessions—and your pocketbook. They can strike at almost any time, anywhere, but you can minimize your personal damage if you prepare. And this is the week for you, your spouse, and your children to sit down and discuss just what you should—and shouldn't—do if you are hit by a severe weather emergency or some other natural disaster.

Above all, work out a preparedness plan. If you live in an area that is prone to extreme weather emergencies, make evacuation plans in advance. After an earthquake or some other natural disaster, roads in and out of the vicinity may be blocked, so identify more than one evacuation route. Teach children how and when to call 911.

If you ever suffer losses from a flood, a hurricane, a twister, or some other natural disaster, you may be able to get considerable help from the government. The Federal Emergency Management Agency (FEMA) offers several forms of disaster aid—notably, low-interest loans and cash grants up to $13,900. The Small Business Administration (SBA) and the Farmers Home Administration (FHA) also provide low-interest credit to help you repair or replace damaged property. If a natural disaster leaves your home unlivable, FEMA may be able to get you temporary housing.

Floods are the leading weather-related killers; they have caused over 10,000 deaths in the United States since 1900. If you hear that there's a flood danger in your area, keep a battery-operated radio on at all times, to listen for instructions and news reports.

If you're ordered to evacuate or if rising water is threatening, decamp immediately and get to higher ground. Do not try to walk through flowing water that is more than ankle-deep. Do not drive through flooded areas—the most deaths from floods occur among people trying to escape in vehicles.

FEMA notes that family members fairly often are separated from one another during floods—particularly during the day, when adults are at work and children are at school. If you live in a frequently flooded area, have a plan for getting together again. Ask an out-of-state relative or friend to serve as the family contact. After a disaster, it's often easier to call long distance than to get a call through locally. Make sure everyone in the family knows the name, address, and phone number of the contact person.

Keep plenty of disaster supplies on hand, including flashlights, a portable battery-operated radio, and extra batteries; a first-aid kit and manual; any essential medicines that you're going to need; sturdy shoes; emergency food and water; and a hand-operated, nonelectric can opener. Imagine laying in all those cans of food and not being able to open them?

Don't forget cash—lots of it. If electricity is out after a weather emergency, you may not be able to use your credit cards.

Return home only after authorities announce on the radio that your area is safe. Use a flashlight when you enter damaged buildings. Do not use lights or appliances until an electrician has checked the electrical system. Check for gas leaks. If you smell gas or hear a blowing or hissing noise, open a window and quickly leave the building.

The Department of Commerce offers this advice: If you're caught at home when a tornado or some other violent storm is approaching, go to the basement or to an interior room on the lowest floor, such as a closet or bathroom. Stay away from exterior walls or glassy areas. Wrap yourself in overcoats or blankets as protection against flying debris. If you're in a car or a mobile home, abandon the vehicle immediately. That's where most tornado deaths occur.

People in Florida know a thing or two about hurricanes. Here's what the *Tampa Tribune* recommends, if you must evacuate your home to escape any natural disaster:

- Take important papers with you, including your driver's license, special medical information, insurance policies, and an inventory of the property that you're leaving behind.

- Let friends and neighbors know where you're going.
- Lock windows and doors.
- Turn off the electricity at the main breaker.
- Store in your empty appliances the valuables and irreplaceable treasures that you can't take along. Tuck them into your washer or dryer, dishwasher, oven, even your microwave. This will help protect them.
- Put plastic bags over TVs, lamps, and computers.
- Fill new garbage cans with water. Use the water for flushing, bathing, washing clothes, and so forth, when you return.

Disinfect any tap water that you drink or use for cooking or personal cleaning. You must purify water until officials say it's safe. Bring water to a rolling boil or use water purification tablets. Properly stored water should be good for two or three weeks.

If you buy any items after a severe storm, get a receipt. Insurance may cover the cost of emergency food and other items.

Make use of other services. For crisis counseling, ask the American Red Cross, churches, and synagogues. For free legal counseling, check the Young Lawyers Division of the American Bar Association. If you're a veteran, look into any special aid programs offered by the Department of Veterans Affairs. Check with the Internal Revenue Service or a tax accountant to see what tax deductions you may be eligible for.

No homeowners' policy insures against all perils. The most popular type of policy, called HO-3, provides comprehensive coverage for the ordinary homeowner. It will reimburse you not only for fire and windstorm, but also if your water pipes freeze and burst. For protection against losses from floods or earthquakes, you need to seek extra coverage at higher cost.

If you had the foresight to make a written or videotaped inventory of all your possessions (see Week 37: Make a List of All Your Possessions), any claim that you submit will be complete, and your chances of collecting sooner will be promising.

Write a Will That Works

Peeople are living so long these days that you might decide that your ninetieth birthday would be a good day to draft your will. Bad idea. Whatever your adult age, it's wise to have a will. Go to a lawyer this week and write a will, or update the one you have, if it is more than three years old.

As mentioned earlier, you probably will accumulate, during your lifetime, more wealth than you had ever expected to leave to your heirs, thanks to all those IRA and 401(k) funds, and the fruits of a long bull market. That's all the more reason why you would be wise to put in writing just who will, someday, inherit your assets.

To do this, you simply engage a lawyer to draft a will that states your instructions for how your wealth is to be distributed after your demise. You sign it (usually in the presence of witnesses), and you put it in a safe but accessible place. Officials of your state will see to it that your intentions are carried out, through the public process called probate.

More than mere wealth may be at stake. Only if you have a properly executed will or trust can you appoint a guardian for your children or make special provision for an aging relative or a handicapped child. Or a significant other.

And here's another reason to have a valid, unshakable, up-to-date will: No family situation brings on more stress than dividing up Dad's or Mom's estate after a parent dies. One academic study has shown that when no legally binding instructions were left behind, arguments among the heirs were four times as likely to occur.

Some lawyers will draw up your will for $250 to $500, but the cost rises, sometimes steeply, if your finances are complex. Don't be shy about interviewing a prospective lawyer and getting the expected cost in writing.

Lawyers admit that wills are often loss leaders, and they hope to be made executors for the estate. Fees for executors typically are 2 percent to 5 percent, but can run as high as 8 percent of the gross estate. However, you are under no obligation to do more than pay your lawyer for the will.

Here are some do's and don'ts about wills:

- Do hire a lawyer to draft your will—and your spouse's. Yes, you can write a will yourself, using one of the many how-to books, or the forms published by some states. But if you make just one slip, your will may be worthless. Only a lawyer knows what your state will consider a valid document.
- Do get witnesses. Most states do not accept wills or trusts that have not been vouched for by witnesses. Don't ask a beneficiary to be a witness; the will may

be legal, but the beneficiary could lose his or her legacy.

- Do sign only one copy of the will, under the supervision and witness of your attorney, and leave it with him or her. You can make minor changes with amendments at any time.
- Don't put your will in a safe-deposit box. Some states require that safe-deposit boxes be sealed when the holder dies, and it takes time to get the will released.
- Do use percentages rather than dollar amounts when making bequests. If you don't, much can go wrong. Take the sorry case of a man who left all of his $100,000 estate to his beloved sister, except for $10,000 that he willed to his nephew. But when the man died after a long illness, medical bills had shrunk his estate to only $12,000. The nephew got his promised $10,000 but the unfortunate sister collected only $2,000. The man would have been far wiser to have left his nephew 10 percent of the estate. In that case, the sister would have collected $10,800.
- Do review your will at least once every three years— or more often if there is major new tax legislation or a significant change in your family status—and keep it up-to-date. You may want to change some bequests, especially now that new estate tax rules enable you to leave, free of taxes, somewhat more money than before.
- Do revise your will if you move, particularly from a common-law state to a community-property state, or vice versa. In a community-property state, almost

any assets acquired during marriage are jointly owned by both partners—except for gifts and inheritances. In a common-law state, assets are owned by the person who buys them.

You can make small changes without writing a new will. For example, you can switch a beneficiary or change the amount of a bequest. In such cases, your lawyer usually will write a codicil, which must be witnessed and kept with your will. But don't write on the will itself. Such changes may invalidate it, reducing all your careful planning to ashes.

Many people think that creating a will or a trust is unnecessary because their surviving spouse will automatically inherit everything. But this is true in only some states, and only if the assets were acquired during the marriage and were not gifts to or inheritances of one spouse.

In most states, the law will make your surviving spouse share your estate with your children, siblings, or parents—unless you declare otherwise in a will. And because assets left to anyone other than a spouse face heavy estate taxes if they are more than $675,000, the federal government can become an unintended heir to your estate.

Remember: Even if you are a middle-income earner, you may be building up substantial—and eventually highly taxable—assets. These include your 401(k), 403(b), IRA, SEP, Keogh, and other tax-deferred plans; your company stock purchase, savings, and pension plans; your private savings and investments; your house and its furnishings (and any other real estate); your cars, art objects, jewelry, and other personal property; your cash in a bank or elsewhere; your share of any business you partly or wholly own; your copy-rights; and your claims against others.

The only thing not considered part of your taxable estate is an asset that you have given away completely and permanently—one that you no longer control and from which you get no benefits.

That's why it pays to give away, to your children and other heirs whom you want someday to inherit your estate, as much as you legally (and comfortably) can during your lifetime. Make a solid will to divide up your assets, and ask your lawyer whether you have enough assets to set up a trust that may deflect some estate taxes.

Choose a Guardian for Your Children

Wills aren't just for distributing property. If you're a parent of young children, the most important thing you must pass on in your will is the responsibility of caring for your kids—and their inheritances—if you and your spouse die before they reach adulthood.

Die without a will, and a court will appoint a guardian for your offspring. If you write a will, you and your spouse can make that important choice.

But note that a guardian whom you name in your will can refuse to accept that heavy responsibility. Discuss the matter with the person whom you would like to do the job, before writing his or her name into your will.

You may appoint two guardians if you wish—one to care for your children and another to manage their money. Be aware, however, that the guardian of your children's inheritance must submit periodic formal reports to the court and may even have to obtain a judge's approval before making large expenditures on private schools or orthodontia.

WEEK

40

See Which Trusts Are Right for You

The rising debate in Congress over whether to reduce or even eliminate the estate tax has prompted many Americans to consider how they can further protect the value of their estate. One way that is gaining in popularity is to set up a trust.

There are four major reasons why people—ordinary people, not just the fabulously wealthy—establish trusts. You and your spouse, if you're married, should have a heart-to-heart with each other, and then with an expert lawyer, to determine whether you should create one or more trusts.

Contrary to popular wisdom, trusts aren't fraught with complexity, nor are they useful only to the leisure class. A trust is simply a contract between a grantor—in this case, you—and a trustee. The trustee holds legal title to the trust property and follows the rules that you set down in the trust document that you and your lawyer draft.

The trustee you select may be a financially astute and trustworthy relative or friend, or you could hire a professional.

The pros—in banks, trust companies, brokerage houses, mutual fund firms, and law and accounting firms—charge a wide range of fees, but most use a sliding scale. For example, a bank might charge 1.5 percent of a trust's assets up to $500,000, then 1.2 percent of the next $500,000, and so on. Most financial institutions won't handle trusts of less than $100,000 (that figure rises to $250,000 in the New York City area).

Now for those four reasons to establish a trust:

1. To preserve and protect your estate from the depredations of the Internal Revenue Service.
2. To avoid probate—the often messy and very public scene in which a court tests and evaluates how your assets are passed on to your beneficiaries after your death. In many states, notably in the Northeast, probate can be costly, slow, and complex. Often, charges Yale Law Professor John Langbein, a trust expert, the process is "corrupt," meaning that the court fees are outrageous and your assets might not be distributed in a manner that you would have approved. By establishing an *intervivos trust*—a trust that is independent of a will—you can avoid the publicity and clamor of probate, because everything is settled out of court.
3. To ensure that a prudent, expert third party—but not your spouse, children, or other beneficiaries—will manage the assets in your estate after your demise.
4. To anticipate incapacity, for example, from Alzheimer's disease.

If you're thinking of setting up a trust, here are the key types you should investigate.

Bypass Trust

This document, a bypass or credit shelter trust, is deservedly popular among married couples. Each spouse gets a lifetime exemption from federal estate and gift taxes. The present exemption of $675,000 is scheduled to rise to $1,000,000 in 2006. Make sure that BOTH of you use your exemptions. You do this by setting up a bypass trust in each of your wills.

Let's say that when you meet your Maker, you have a taxable net worth of $2,000,000. If you leave it all directly to your spouse, he or she will get the full $2,000,000—free of estate or gift taxes, thanks to the marital exclusion. So far, so fine.

The trouble is that, when the surviving spouse dies, only $675,000 can pass tax-free to the children or other heirs. That is the current estate and gift tax exemption. The remainder of what you have passed on—$1,325,000—will be fully taxed.

You can prevent much of this taxation by creating a bypass trust and putting into it the maximum of $675,000. After you die, your spouse can draw interest and dividend income from that trust and even dip into its principal if needed.

When your spouse eventually dies, $675,000 of his or her assets, plus whatever the value of the bypass trust is, will go to your heirs, tax-free. Now that's smart tax planning.

Q-TIP Trust

If you don't want to leave a large estate to your spouse outright, you could set up a Q-TIP—it stands for a qualified terminable interest property trust (I never thought you'd ask).

Property that you place in a Q-TIP qualifies for the 100 percent marital deduction, and your spouse gets lifetime interest from the trust. But when your spouse dies, the principal goes to your chosen heirs, thereby keeping your legacy out of the hands of a gold digger, should the surviving spouse remarry. The Q-TIP is also popular with people who have remarried and wish to ensure that their assets will ultimately go to their heirs.

Life Insurance Trust

Normally, your insurance proceeds are part of your estate and are subject to tax. But you can shelter them by transferring ownership of your policies to an irrevocable life insurance trust (the "irrevocable" means that you can't alter its provisions). You can name your children or other heirs as the trust's beneficiaries. When you die, they collect your insurance proceeds, untaxed.

A life insurance trust will work only if it meets a number of conditions. The trustee whom you name—not you—should pay the policy premiums. Also, if you die within three years of setting up a trust, your insurance will become part of your taxable estate. So, your attorney should insert in the trust a clause stating that should you die within three years, your insurance proceeds will go directly to your spouse or into a trust for him or her.

Charitable Remainder Trust

Through this type of trust, you give away, during your lifetime, stocks, bonds, mutual funds, real estate, or other valuable property to a charity or a religious or public service organization. But you continue to collect interest payments or other income from it until the trust ends—usually, when you die. Another benefit is that you get an immediate tax deduction for your donation. The higher the return you earn from the trust, the smaller your tax deduction. Older donors get richer tax breaks than younger ones because they stand to collect income from their trusts over a shorter life expectancy.

Charitable Lead Trust

If you don't need additional income and want to avoid estate tax on stocks or other property that you think will appreciate, set up a charitable lead trust instead of a charitable remainder trust. When you die, the property goes into an irrevocable trust that pays income to your favorite charity or pro bono organization for a limited period of time—typically, for more than ten years. After that, the assets in the trust pass to your heirs. This was the kind of trust that Jacqueline Kennedy Onassis used, to brilliant effect, to give immediate support to her favorite charities and simultaneously preserve a large share of her assets, which her heirs will collect 24 years after her death.

Generation-Skipping and Tax Trust

This enables you to give assets to your grandchildren or great-grandchildren instead of to your children so that you can reduce the number of times your estate is whacked by the estate tax. The first $1,030,000 ($2,060,000 if spouses give jointly) that is transferred to a generation-skipping tax trust escapes the punishing 55 percent federal generation-skipping tax.

Revocable Living Trust

You may have heard from friends that you should create a revocable living trust instead of a will, so that your estate avoids probate. They may have a point—if your state makes probate a lengthy and expensive ordeal. But don't assume that it does.

Find out your state's rules covering probate, and decide whether it makes sense for you to draft a revocable living trust, or some other form of trust, in order to dodge probate and perhaps achieve some other goals.

Probate is less painful than the norm in 21 states and the District of Columbia, which permit so-called unsupervised or independent administration of estates of any size. Those 21 states are: Alabama, Alaska, Arizona, Colorado, Georgia, Hawaii, Idaho, Illinois, Maine, Michigan, Minnesota, Missouri, Nebraska, New Jersey, New Mexico, North Dakota, Pennsylvania, South Dakota, Texas, Utah, and Washington.

When a court admits your will to probate in those states, the executor of your will completes all required paperwork, pays your debts, and distributes your assets to your heirs without having to get a judge's approval. He or she then sends your estate's final accounting to your heirs and to a probate clerk, but not to a judge. The whole process typically takes only three to five months, versus nine months for supervised probate.

Probate is costlier in some states than in others. It can devour anywhere from 1 percent to a frightening 8 percent of your estate, depending on the size of the estate and, perhaps, the complexity of your will. (In some states, executors are allowed to charge higher fees for complex wills.) You must also take into account that lawyers typically charge $1,500 to $2,000 to draft a revocable living trust, compared with only $250 or so for a simple will.

Here's how a revocable living trust works. Your attorney draws up a document in which you transfer ownership of real estate, securities, or other assets to a trustee who manages them for beneficiaries you name. You can retain control of the assets you put in a trust, receive income from them, change the trust's provisions, or end it. In most states, you can even serve alone as your own trustee.

After your death, the trust's assets can go to your heirs, or the assets can remain intact while the income from them goes to your heirs. Either way, property in the trust avoids probate.

Living trusts have another advantage. If you ever become incapacitated, a successor trustee, whom you name in the trust, can take over the management of your money for you.

Parents of minors may establish living trusts but they still need simple wills, chiefly because a guardian for kids can't be named in a trust. And everyone who has a living trust also needs a "pour-over will," stipulating that any property you forgot to put in your trust should go there after your death. Those assets will have to go through probate, but the process shouldn't take long or cost much, assuming that you remembered to shift most of your assets to a living trust before your death. The reason: Most states have stripped-down probate procedures for very modest estates that take only a day or two to complete.

Whether you choose to write a will or create a living trust, ask your lawyer to draw up a living will and a durable power of attorney for health care.

In a living will, you make known your preferences for medical treatment in life-or-death situations, so that your relatives and doctors can act accordingly. A durable power of attorney for health care gives a trusted person, whom you name, legal authority to state your preferences for medical treatment if, say, you're knocked unconscious or become comatose and unable to communicate.

WEEK

41

Grant a Power of Attorney

Here's something you can do this week to help protect you and your family: Grant a power of attorney. This fairly simple legal document entitles someone whom you choose to handle your financial affairs in case you cannot. If you are required to do extended travel overseas, especially in dangerous or remote areas, or if you suffer a disabling illness or accident, it's reassuring to know that someone whom you consider capable and trustworthy can—and will—manage your affairs.

The person to whom you grant a power of attorney can do such things as pay your bills, make investment decisions, and handle your personal finances.

A lawyer can draw up a power of attorney document for you; usually, the fee is $100 to $200. It's wiser to enlist a legal pro than to try to create this document yourself, using a standard form that you can buy in stationery shops. Your financial institutions may refuse to comply with third-party boilerplate forms. Each state also has its own laws and court rulings about how to execute a power of attorney, so it's best to employ a lawyer.

One exception: Ask your banker and stockbroker to let you exercise their own company's durable power of attorney form. Financial institutions can be balky about acknowledging outside attorneys' documents, even though they are perfectly legal.

The person to whom you give a power of attorney can be a family member—or someone you know of but haven't even met yet. You can delegate different people to handle specific aspects of your personal affairs. For example, you can delegate the care and management of your real estate investments to one person, your stocks and bonds to another, and your taxes to yet another.

Don't worry that giving someone a power of attorney will tie your hands. You can specify all sorts of conditions and restrictions under which the power of attorney may operate. A very important fact: As long as you are competent, you can revoke this power at any time.

(Note: The powers of attorney discussed here *cannot* be used to make health care decisions for you or family members. You can address those decisions only by creating a separate health care power of attorney.)

There are two main kinds of powers of attorney:

1. A Special Power of Attorney. This limits the freedom of the designated person by specifying just what he or she may do—for example, handle your banking transactions, enter your safe-deposit boxes, sell or manage your real estate, and make estate-planning decisions, such as starting or operating a trust. But

he or she may not write a will for you. Only you can do that.

2. A General Power of Attorney. This very broad power allows your agent to act on your behalf in a vast variety of matters: those mentioned before, plus making securities investments, buying life insurance and settling claims, applying for government aid programs, filing your tax returns, and much more. Such a power is especially useful when you're traveling to an inaccessible place and need someone to manage all of your affairs during your absence.

As with a living will, you may want certain wishes carried out by the person you designate. You should discuss them with him or her and perhaps record them in a separate written document.

Mike Palermo, an attorney and certified financial planner in Lexington, Kentucky, advises that any power of attorney should explicitly declare that it remains valid at least during the entire period of disability or incapacity.

If you have elderly parents, suggest that they grant a power of attorney to someone, perhaps to yourself. If the time comes when they are unable to conduct their own financial affairs, and they have not given a power of attorney to yourself or someone else, a court may appoint a conservator to make financial decisions on their behalf. Once appointed, this guardian has almost unlimited control over the finances of the incapacitated person (called the *donor* or *principal*)—in this case, one or both of your parents.

The appointed guardian is usually a family member but could be a total stranger. Even the family member designated by the courts might not have the ability or the inclination to act in the donor's best interests. Thus, it is often much better for your parents to pick the person who will exercise the power of attorney.

If your parents resist letting anyone—even you, their own child—mess with their investments, ask them to give you a "springing power of attorney." This specifies the conditions in which you can act on behalf of your mother or father. It might say, for example: "This power of attorney shall become effective only upon the disability or incapacity of the principal, as attested by no fewer than two physicians."

Ease the Estate Tax Bite

You don't have to be a fat cat to worry about estate taxes.

They can bite. Federal estate taxes run from 37 percent (for everything that you leave worth more than $675,000) to 55 percent (for everything in an estate above $3,000,000). Tax expert James Weikart, of New York City, calculates that if you inherit an estate worth $1,000,000, you stand to be hit with a federal estate tax of $125,250. And then—hold on to your hat!—the tax rises sharply from there: the tax is $1,070,250 on an estate worth $3,000,000, and $2,170,250 on an estate of $5,000,000.

But we're not done yet. In addition, many states pile on their own estate taxes.

The prolonged, noninflationary growth and spreading prosperity that most forecasters expect for the United States could so greatly swell the value of your stock-purchase, savings, and pension plans and your tax-deferred retirement plans—not to mention your mutual funds and sundry investments—that your assets would create both a windfall and an estate-tax migraine for your heirs. Even if you are a middle-income earner, you may be building up substantial— and highly taxable—assets.

The 75 million baby boomers are shaping up as America's first Generation of Inheritors. They stand to inherit *trillions* of dollars from their increasingly affluent parents, and, not surprisingly, they would prefer to collect it without taking a haircut from Uncle Sam. And yes, those boomers *do* vote.

Consequently, a clangorous debate has erupted in Congress over whether to end—or at least reduce—what is charmingly known as "the death tax."

My own guess is that this highly contentious, heavily emotional tax will *not* be eliminated—there's too much worry that we might build a dynastic society of elites—but the tax will be reduced. In any case, you'll be hearing more about this issue during the coming months.

Pay heed to the arguments and the outcome. If you're like most people, you're worth more than you think. Just ask those friendly tax collectors at the IRS. When calculating your taxable estate, they count in *everything* you own: all your stocks, bonds, mutual funds, and other investments; the assets you have accumulated in IRAs, 401(k)s, 403(b)s, profit sharing, and other tax-deferred savings plans; your house or apartment and its furnishings, and any other real estate you own; your cars, artwork, jewelry, and other personal property; your cash in the bank or elsewhere; your share of any business you wholly or partly own; your copyrights and claims against others; and on and on.

To legitimately reduce the estate tax, it makes sense for you to reduce the size of your estate. This week, make a plan to give away as much as you legally and comfortably can during your lifetime. Give it to your children and other heirs whom you want someday to inherit what you have earned, invested, and created.

It's nice to make gifts to your spouse for the sake of love alone. But you don't have to worry about giving gifts to him or her to avoid taxes. If you leave this world before your spouse does, all your assets will flow to her or him *free* of estate taxes. Your spouse is the only person to whom you can make unlimited gifts without paying a gift tax—provided he or she is a U.S. citizen.

A huge problem occurs when heirs do not have the money readily available to pay estate taxes. All too often, this happens when the main asset they inherit is a small business or real estate. Your children may have to sell the business (or other asset) at distress prices. No wonder so few small businesses are successfully passed to younger generations.

If you think that your estate will someday be clobbered by federal estate taxes, consult an attorney this week. Seek one who is an expert in estate matters, not a general practitioner. The charge of $100 to $300 an hour will probably be well worth it.

The lawyer may tell you that a sound way to provide money to pay the estate tax is to buy life insurance—specifically, a "second-to-die" or "survivorship" policy. The premium is relatively low because the policy pays off only after *both* spouses have died. The death benefit incurs no estate tax, provided that you put the policy into an *irrevocable* life insurance trust. Either your heirs pay the annual premium, or you and your spouse do—so long as the policy is not owned by the insured. The latter practice is more common, but then you have to declare these premium payments as gifts to the beneficiaries of the policy, who are almost always your children. You will have to pay gift taxes if your payments exceed the gift tax limits.

Example: A married couple, ages 65 and 70, buy a $1,000,000 second-to-die life policy from an insurance company that has high grades from ratings firms such as A.M. Best or Standard & Poor's. If both spouses pass the insurance company's medical tests and get the top health ratings, the annual premium should be about $25,000. This assumes that the policy is a "blend" of approximately 50 percent whole life and 50 percent term insurance. The price is lower—at least for several years—if the insurance is entirely a term policy and therefore is pure insurance and builds up no cash value. The price is higher if it's entirely a whole life policy, which builds up cash value like a savings account. The insured couple can make gifts of the $25,000 premium to the beneficiaries of the policy.

That $25,000 is a fistful of money—especially when you have to pay it every year. But remember: It is buying you $1,000,000 worth of protection, and your heirs someday may need every nickel of it to pay the estate taxes. Naturally, the premiums are lower if the insured couple are younger than our hypothetical 65- and 70-year-old couple, and the premiums are higher if the insured couple has less-than-sterling health ratings.

The description of a trust as *irrevocable* means just what it implies: You cannot change the rules later on. Once you put any assets into an *irrevocable* trust, you give up all control of them. They stay in the trust until you die, and then they are given to the beneficiaries whom you have named. If one of those beneficiaries turns out to be a wastrel, or chooses to spend the money not for college but for cults or crack, tough luck.

But, almost certainly, you have raised your children well, and they will turn out to be terrific. Do all you can so that they will not be hurt by the punishing estate tax.

Open an IRA—or
a Roth IRA

Once regarded as a tax shelter for blue-collar Americans, the Individual Retirement Account (IRA) has been converted by Congress in recent years into a terrific, tax-saving deal for a broader range of middle- and upper-middle-income people. Even if you and your spouse have a pension or tax-deferred retirement savings plan such as a 401(k) where you work, or a Keogh, you can open an IRA and start reaping its tax benefits. Every year, you can deposit up to $2,000 from earnings into your account, and your spouse can do the same—even if he or she doesn't hold a paying job. That money grows and grows, free of taxes, until you withdraw it—usually, when you retire.

Just about everybody should have an IRA, as long as he or she can afford to contribute to it after stuffing the maximum into employer-sponsored retirement savings programs and special plans for the self-employed (some of which can be better deals than IRAs).

You can contribute to an IRA only if you (or your spouse) have earned income from a job or receive alimony. You can open and contribute to any number of such accounts at a bank or credit union, a brokerage firm, an insurance company, or a mutual fund company. You can have as many accounts as you wish, as long as your total combined contributions to them don't exceed $2,000 a year. Finally, you can open your IRA and make your contribution for the year as late as the date you file your taxes for income earned during that year—April 15.

Here are the basic rules of the three different types of IRAs.

1. *Traditional deductible IRAs.* You can fully deduct your $2,000 contribution from your current income if neither you nor your spouse is covered by an employer-sponsored pension plan. If you do have such a plan—whether or not you are vested—you can still *fully* deduct your IRA contribution as long as your adjusted gross income (AGI) is less than $31,000 if you're single, or $51,000 if you're married and file a joint tax return. You can *partially* deduct your IRA contribution if your AGI is $31,001 to $41,000 if you're single, $51,001 to $61,000 if you're married and filing jointly.

An employed spouse not covered by a pension plan at work—but married to an employed person who is covered— may deduct the full $2,000 IRA contribution if the couple's AGI is below $150,000, and may deduct part of it if the AGI is $150,000 to $160,000.

You can invest your IRA in stocks, bonds, mutual funds, bank certificates, and other financial instruments, but not in art, collectibles, or precious metals, except for certain U.S. and state coins.

If you take money out of your account before age 59½, you usually will be socked with a 10 percent tax penalty, plus regular income taxes on the amount withdrawn. Among the exceptions: There's no penalty if you withdraw money to pay medical expenses that exceed 7.5 percent of your AGI, or to pay for qualified higher-education expenses, or to buy a first home. (In this last case, the penalty-free withdrawal can't exceed $10,000.)

You cannot contribute to a deductible IRA after you reach age 70½, even if you are still working. You must have begun withdrawals by April 1 in the year after you reached 70½, or you'll be hit with a draconian penalty: 50 percent of the amount you should have withdrawn, based on government projections of your life expectancy. And you must still make the withdrawal and pay income taxes on it.

2. *Nondeductible traditional IRAs.* If you can't deduct your contribution from your taxable income, you can open a nondeductible account, which still can be an excellent tax saver because your money will grow, tax-deferred, until you withdraw it. Tax-free compounding can enable your money to expand remarkably fast. If you put away $2,000 every January and it grows at a rather modest average of 8 percent annually, you will have about:

$31,290 after 10 years,
$98,945 after 20 years,
$244,690 after 30 years, and
$559,562 after 40 years.

At a 10 percent rate of return—slightly less than stocks' historic growth over the past 70 years—your investment would double in seven years and reach $126,005 in 20 years.

All the other rules of deductible IRAs apply to non-deductible ones. You can invest in financial instruments but not art, collectibles, or precious metals, except for certain U.S. and state coins. You generally suffer the 10 percent penalty for taking money out before age 59½, and you must begin withdrawals by April 1 the year after you reach 70½.

There are some drawbacks to nondeductible IRAs. Chief among them: They require extra record keeping; you must carefully track the amount of your nondeductible contributions. This money won't be taxed when you begin withdrawals. You will, however, have to pay taxes on your account's earnings. Worse, you can't simply decide to withdraw only your nontaxable contributions to keep your taxes simple. Instead, the IRA will regard each withdrawal as partly tax-free and partly taxable in the same proportion as the taxable and nontaxable money in your account. It'll be up to you to make the calculation each year. Also, nondeductible contributions must be reported annually on IRS Form 8606, which you attach to your tax return.

3. *Roth IRAs.* Working Americans in the past several years have become eligible for Roth IRAs, named after their chief proponent, Senator William Roth (R–Del.). They should be of keen interest to people who don't expect their tax brackets to fall after retirement.

Unlike many traditional IRAs, Roth IRAs do not allow you to deduct your yearly contributions from your taxable income. With a Roth account, you contribute after-tax money, rather than pretax money, to your account. But if you leave your money in your account for at least five years, all your withdrawals after you reach 59$\frac{1}{2}$ will be *tax-free*.

These accounts are available to workers with AGIs of up to $95,000 if single, or $150,000 if married and filing jointly. Reduced contributions are available to singles with AGIs of $95,000 to $110,000, and to joint filers with AGIs of $150,000 to $160,000. (The income limits will rise with inflation in future years.)

As with deductible IRAs, you can invest your Roth contributions in stocks, bonds, and other financial instruments but not art, collectibles, or precious metals, except for certain U.S. and state coins. Also, you'll generally be hit with the 10 percent penalty plus regular income taxes on withdrawals before age 59$\frac{1}{2}$, unless you die, become disabled, or use the money to buy a qualified first home.

Which kind of IRA should you open? If your income exceeds the limits, your only choice is a nondeductible IRA. But if you qualify for both a deductible IRA and a Roth account, financial planners recommend that you choose the Roth if you expect your tax bracket to remain unchanged—or even to rise—in retirement.

But what if you already have a deductible IRA? Should you convert it to a Roth account—an option that is available only if your AGI is below $100,000, whether you're single or married?

The problem is that you have to pay ordinary income taxes on the profits you withdraw from your traditional IRA. Still, doing just that makes sense for many people who would gain greatly by being able—eventually—to make tax-free withdrawals. You'll stand to come out ahead in the long run if:

- You don't have to tap your IRA funds to pay the tax due on the rollover to a Roth, or sell other assets and incur big capital-gains taxes.
- You're relatively young—that is, you have a lot of years to make up for the quick tax hit.
- You expect your tax bracket to stay the same or go higher after retirement. (In estimating your taxable income in retirement, don't forget to count your pension, investment income, and Social Security benefits.)

But a Roth is like an IRA on steroids. True, the contributions you make to it are not immediately tax-deductible. You make your contributions in after-tax dollars. But everything you take out after age $59\frac{1}{2}$—all the accumulated principal and interest and dividends and capital gains—is totally tax-free. So, when you retire, you can enjoy all the money in your account, without handing a big chunk over to Uncle Sam.

And unlike with a regular IRA, you're not forced to make mandatory withdrawals after age $70\frac{1}{2}$. Indeed, you can keep on contributing no matter how old you are. The money can stay in your Roth and continue to build. You can even pass it on to your heirs, and they can inherit your Roth IRA income-tax-free.

Put another way: Unlike many traditional IRAs, Roth IRAs do not allow you to deduct your yearly contributions from your taxable income. But that may well be less important to you than the fact that you can withdraw your total contributions and the earnings on them entirely tax-free—*provided* that your Roth IRA is at least five years old, *and* you are at least 59½ years old, or you have gone on to meet your maker, in which case your heirs will collect.

A Roth IRA is particularly attractive to young adults and others who are in lower tax brackets now than they probably will be later on, when they retire and begin to withdraw their IRA money. Put another way: If you expect to jump into higher tax brackets during your working career, a Roth IRA—with its tax-free withdrawals—is a sensible choice.

To open a Roth IRA, just get in touch with your friendly bank, brokerage house, or mutual fund. You then can make annual contributions of up to $2,000 if you are single and have an adjusted gross income of $95,000 or less, or if you are married and filing jointly and have an AGI of $150,000 or less.

Given their flexibility, investing your IRA is like shopping in a well-stocked financial supermarket. My own favorite repository for an IRA, particularly for young people who are confident of the future and willing to take sensible risk, is a no-load growth mutual fund that invests in blue-chip stocks or mimics the Standard & Poor's 500 stock index. Better yet, choose a fund company with a wide array of funds so that you can more easily transfer your money to faster-growing ones or diversify among different types as your retirement cache grows in those taxable and nonadvantaged accounts.

Beyond that, my advice on investing your IRA money is the same as you've read in Week 25: Choose the Right

Investment Mix. But in determining your allocation, be sure to count *all* your invested assets—those in taxable *and* tax-advantaged accounts.

No matter what type of IRA you have—or even if you maintain all three types of accounts—your money will grow much faster if you put in your contributions as early each year as possible. Let's say you contribute the $2,000 maximum but procrastinate until every April 15. If your investment earns 10 percent annually, you will have $114,500 in 20 years. But if you make that contribution every January 1, you will wind up with $11,450 *more.*

If you can't afford to make your annual contribution all at once, you can make smaller, periodic contributions with most banks, brokerages, and mutual funds. You can even skip a year, but you can't make up the missed contribution in future years. Besides opening as many IRAs as you please (watch out, though, for multiple fees!), you can transfer your money from one account to another as often as you wish.

The $2,000-a-year limit on IRAs probably will be increased in the near-term future. Republicans in Congress—notably, Delaware Senator William Roth, who devised the Roth IRA—want to expand the annual limit, in stages, to $5,000. Meanwhile, you may want to enlarge your tax-sheltered retirement fund by investing as well in a 401(k): Yes, you *can* have both an IRA and a 401(k).

You also may want to look into the new Education IRAs. They let parents, relatives, and friends contribute up to $500 a year toward the cost of a child's college education. Contributions to the account are not tax-deductible. But you can avoid ever paying any taxes on the profits in the account, as long as withdrawals are used to pay for tuition, room, board, and other qualified education costs.

The money in an Education IRA surely won't cover the entire cost of a child's studies, but it will provide a head start. And, putting money in one of these accounts will not limit your ability to contribute to traditional IRAs.

Seek a Special Shelter If You're Self-Employed

Now is the time to benefit from two highly advantageous tax-deferred retirement accounts, if you are self-employed. You can work for yourself—full time, part time, or freelance. You can work at one job for an employer but still contribute your earnings from a second, sideline business, as long as it qualifies as self-employment. Among those eligible are most actors, carpenters, dentists, doctors, freelance writers, lawyers, plumbers, small-business owners, waiters, and self-employed moonlighters of any kind. The two tax shelters for which these people qualify are Keogh Plans and Simplified Employee Pensions (SEPs).

In general, SEPs are simpler to set up and administer than the maddeningly complex Keoghs. But you can shelter more money in Keoghs, which makes them more compelling to high earners and procrastinators who have dallied until their mid-forties, or later, before starting to save in earnest for their retirement. We'll begin our discussion with the Keogh Plans, which can give you more bang for your bucks.

Keogh Plans

Basically, there are four kinds of Keoghs, but before we describe their complicated differences, let's explain what they have in common:

- Keogh accounts must be established by December 31 of the year for which you are making a contribution. But you can postpone actually putting the money into the account until you file your tax return—usually, on April 15 of the following year, or October 15 if you get an extension.
- The rules governing all Keoghs are quite daunting, though the financial institution where you keep your account—for example, a bank, brokerage, or mutual fund company—can help you avoid running afoul of Internal Revenue Service regulations. Still, you may want to hire a knowledgeable accountant or lawyer to help you set up your plan.
- In certain complex situations, Keogh holders may have to file a special report with the IRS. To check whether you must, see IRS Publication S60.
- You can put up to $2,000 a year in a tax-deferred Individual Retirement Account, in addition to contributing the maximum (explained below) to your Keogh.
- You generally must wait until you reach age 59½ to take money out of your Keogh. You'll owe a penalty— 10 percent of the withdrawn amount—plus regular income taxes if you take it out earlier.
- You can postpone starting withdrawals until April 1 of the year after the one in which you turn 70½. If

you're then still earning self-employment income, you can continue to contribute to your Keogh.

- If you die before beginning withdrawals, your beneficiary may elect to take all the money either (1) within five years, or (2) over his or her lifetime. If you have already begun to take money out of your account, your beneficiary will continue to receive payments on the same schedule. (Warning: Be sure to choose a term-certain distribution, to ensure that you get the full benefit out of the plan. Before you make your first distribution from your Keogh, contact the institution that holds your plan and ask how to make an election for this type of distribution. Otherwise, whatever amount is left in your account will go to the government when you or your beneficiary dies.)

Here are the pluses and minuses of all four types of Keoghs, starting with the three that are grouped in the category of *defined-contribution plans* because, in each case, you set the size of your contribution.

1. *Profit-sharing.* This account gives you maximum flexibility. You decide each year whether to put money in your plan, and how much: up to a maximum of 15 percent of your "net" self-employment income, or $25,500, whichever is less. If you also have a money-purchase plan, the limit rises to $30,000. (The dollar maximum rises annually, in step with inflation.) "Net" means your income minus the Keogh deduction.

An example may clarify the rule for you. Let's say you earn $50,000 from moonlighting. You can put up to 15 percent of that sum, minus the contribution, into your Keogh.

This works out to a maximum contribution of $6,520, which is 13.04 percent of your total income, or 15 percent of your income minus the contribution.

2. *Money-purchase.* This plan lets you put more money into your account each year—up to 25 percent of your "net" self-employment earnings, or $42,500 for income earned in 2000, whichever is less. (Again, "net" means your earnings minus your contribution; the actual maximum amounts to 20 percent of your total earnings.)

But you pay a price for this larger maximum: When you open your account, you state the percentage of earnings you will contribute annually, and you must continue doing so year after year, even if you're financially hard-pressed and need the money for another purpose.

3. *Hybrid.* This is essentially a profit-sharing Keogh combined with a money-purchase plan. You can therefore commit to putting an easily manageable percentage of your earnings each year into the money-purchase plan, and whatever you can afford into the profit-sharing plan. The combined contributions can't exceed 25 percent of "net" earnings, or $30,000 for 2000 earnings, whichever is less. For example, you might decide to put 7 percent of your "net" earnings into the first plan each year, and, whenever profits are bountiful, 18 percent into the second plan.

4. *Defined-benefit plan.* With this type of Keogh, your contribution limit can be much higher than with the types of plans we've just described. In fact, a defined-benefit Keogh allows some people to put away *all* of their self-employment income.

With such an account, you promise yourself a retirement benefit of some fixed amount each month, beginning between the ages of 59½ and 70½ and continuing for the rest of your life. Then, you have an actuary calculate how much you must contribute each year to fund that pension, depending on your age and your life expectancy. Every year, you must report your actuary's calculation to the IRS.

The downside of a defined-benefit plan is that your actuary must repeat the calculation every year, and you must put into your account the amount he or she estimates—even in years when your business loses money or only breaks even. If you skip contributing to your plan for two years, it could be terminated. Thus, defined-benefit Keoghs are best for high earners who have put off beginning their retirement saving until, say, their mid-forties or even their fifties or sixties.

To avoid a Keogh's paperwork, many self-employed people open *SEPs,* which are like an expanded IRA. Instead of a paltry $2,000, your annual contribution to a SEP can equal 15 percent of your "net" earnings or $24,000, whichever is lower. (In some rare cases, that total can be as high as $30,000.) In addition, as with an IRA or a profit-sharing Keogh, you can vary the amount of your contribution from year to year or even skip it when your income dips or you have a more pressing need for money. SEPs are exempt from Keoghs' annual reporting requirements; indeed, with a SEP, your only paperwork is the one- or two-page form you must fill out and submit to the financial institution where you establish your account.

SEPs have another advantage over Keoghs: You can open your account and make your contribution at any time before you file your tax return for that year.

No matter what kind of tax-deferred retirement account you open, make your annual contribution to it as early in the year as possible. Over 20 or 30 years, the compounding of earnings on early contributions can add tens of thousands of dollars to your account.

How should you invest the money in your Keogh or SEP? Your strategy should match your needs and goals. If your Keogh or SEP will provide most of your retirement income, diversify to reduce your risk, and stick with large-company stocks (or mutual funds that hold them) and with top-rated bonds. But if most of your retirement income will come from elsewhere—say, a pension from your principal employer—you might shoot for higher capital gains with more speculative growth stocks or funds and perhaps with some high-yielding, lower-quality bonds.

Buy—and Lease Back—
Your Parents' House

I'm sure you gave Mom a terrific present for last Mother's Day, but here's an extraordinary gift you might consider for *next* Mother's Day. If you have aging parents, why not buy them a house or a condo—and lease it right back to them? That's a wonderful way for you to help them, and, at the same time, enjoy the juicy tax benefits of being a landlord. You can take big deductions for mortgage interest, maintenance, and depreciation.

Better yet, buy your parents' present house and rent it back to them. That way, they get a bundle of cash and you collect regular rent *and* reap all those deductions. Remember, when they sell their house, your parents may get to exclude up to $500,000 of the gain from their taxable income—or $250,000 if only one of them is still living.

The IRS insists that you charge your kin a fair market rent. You can easily document that by asking a local real estate broker for a written estimate of the rent the property should command. You *and* your parents have to sign a formal lease and keep careful records of the rental payments.

You can make much the same buy-and-lease-back arrangement with another generation in your family—your grown children. This may be a particularly nice deal for newlyweds.

Many parents are also managing to make money on their kids' college education by buying a house in the child's college town and renting it to the child *plus* a number of his or her classmates. Again, be sure you charge a fair market rent to get a passing grade from the IRS. If you hire your child as the building superintendent, you can give him or her a rent rebate.

Make sure, however, that your child won't be reluctant to collect rent from his or her pals. Your child is, in effect, standing in for you as the landlord's agent, and it can be demanding to be a landlord. In any case, many college towns are becoming magnets for development, so buying a house there can be an excellent investment.

Calculate What You Will Need in Retirement

Keep this happy fact in mind: Life spans are lengthening—dramatically. You probably can look forward not only to a longer average life but also to better health than your forebears. As a consequence, you may well spend almost as many years in retirement as on the job. But that means you will have to put away more than you may have originally estimated, so that your eventual retirement will be fun, not a dollar-squeezing drag. Half to two-thirds of your retirement money most likely will have to come from your own savings and investments.

This is a good week to consider how much money you will need for a secure retirement. Begin with the knowledge that you won't require as much as your final year's pay on the job. Your work-related expenses will disappear, your tax bill stands to decline, and you may not be putting part of your income into retirement savings any longer. So, to maintain your standard of living, your pension, your investment and savings income, and your Social Security benefit must add up to 70 percent to 80 percent of your final year's salary.

The way to accumulate that much income is to save and invest more today. Hewitt Associates, a compensation consulting firm, points out how much you can earn, over time, if you put away just slightly more than you may be saving now.

Assume that you're age 30 and earn $40,000 a year. Assume also that you put only 1 percent of your pay in a tax-deferring 401(k) plan, and your employer contributes 50 cents for each dollar you invest. If your pay rises 6 percent each year and your investments earn an average of 8 percent annually, you would retire at age 60 with a nest egg of just under $130,000. If you then bought an annuity from an insurance company, based on a life expectancy of 79 years, the annuity would pay you $14,500 a year.

If, however, you were to put away not just 1 percent but a full 6 percent of your salary, you would leave at age 60 with just over $777,000. You then could buy an annuity paying you $87,000 a year—the equivalent of 45 percent of your final five years' pay.

You may well need every bit of that amount because, if you have a company pension, it may pay you less than you expect. Remember that your pension tends to shrink when you change jobs often, and, these days, there's a lot of musical chairs in the job market. Also, the calculations for most pension plans are based on a presumption that you will retire at age 65 and that you'll take your pension payments as a single-life annuity. But what if you retire at age 60 instead of age 65, as more and more people are doing?

Many employers then cut the benefits by one-third, or by one-half if you depart at age 55.

Looked at another way: Traditional pension plans often pay you only 30 percent of your final five-year average compensation if you retire at age 60. Even loyal employees who have spent their career at one firm and leave at age 65 get only about 40 percent to 45 percent of their income when they retire.

You may well have to forget about that *single-life* annuity. If you are married when you retire, the law requires that your spouse receive payments from your pension in case you should die before she or he does. But there's a cost for this extra protection. Your pension payouts will be somewhat less than they would be under an annuity covering only a single life.

Here's a tip: Check the benefits office where you work, or ask an accountant, for a picture of your retirement benefits. How much do you stand to collect, and when? Will you be better off to take the money in a lump sum or in monthly payments for life?

And how much Social Security can you look forward to? You qualify for Social Security benefits as early as age 62 if you have held a job and paid Social Security taxes for at least 10 years. But retiring at 62 will cost you 20 percent of what you could claim if you wait till age 65, which the Social Security Administration currently considers "full" retirement age (for people born before 1937).

For an official estimate of your future benefits, call Social Security at 1-800-772-1213 and follow the instructions. The agency will send you a form that will help you calculate your benefits. Its questions are easy to answer; you can ask for estimated retirement amounts at various ages from 62 to 70. (Between full retirement age and 70, postponed benefits rise handsomely in terms of monthly income.) A few weeks after returning the form, you will receive a Social Security Statement. Just remember, the figures will be in today's dollars.

Whether you plan to leave the paid workforce in 10 years or in 30, you and your spouse should sit down now with paper and pencil (or at the PC) and note when you think you want to retire, where you want to live, and what you want to do. Regardless of the national averages, you may need far more than 80 percent of your current income. You may want to take frequent trips abroad. Or sail your yacht. Or maintain a seaside or slopeside second home. You may have elderly parents you must help support. Or you may want to leave your children sizable inheritances.

On the other hand, you may be so frugal that you can live on 50 percent or less of your preretirement income. The U.S. Bureau of Retirement Statistics says Americans over age 65 spend 25 percent to 40 percent less than younger folks do on food, clothing, housing, transportation, and other day-to-day expenses. Medical bills are an exception, but Medicare helps and they probably won't cut deeply into your budget until you are in your eighties.

Even if you have been conscientiously putting money aside for retirement, you and your spouse would be wise to set a long-term savings goal *now*. You have no other way of knowing whether you're saving too little, too much, or—cross your fingers!—just enough. If you're two or more decades away from retirement, your plans are likely to be vague. If you're that young, however, you have one powerful advantage: Time is on your side. One dollar saved today will be worth $10.06 in 30 years, assuming a modest 8 percent annual before-tax return. (That's the historic average return for a conservative mix of stocks, bonds, and cash.)

People only a decade away from retirement are likely to have much clearer ideas of what they want to do. But they'll gain less from investment growth. In 10 years, a dollar invested at 8 percent will be worth only $2.16. Late-starters must work harder to accumulate enough savings for a worry-free retirement, but don't despair!

Start out by determining—or at least making an educated guess at—your lifestyle in retirement, using Worksheet 1, on pages 316–318. Of course, retirees' spending patterns change as they grow older—for example, medical and prescription bills typically rise, and spending on travel declines. But, Worksheet 1 will help you forecast your spending in retirement.

Then, use Worksheet 2 on pages 319–320 to set your annual savings goal. You should update both worksheets every year to make sure your savings are on track.

Want help? You can hire a financial planner, seek counsel from a financial services company such as Prudential Securities (Phone: 1-800-843-7625; Web: www.prudential .com), Vanguard (Phone: 1-800-662-7447; Web: www.van-guard.com), or Charles Schwab (1-800-435-4000), or use one of the Internet websites listed in the box on page 315.

When you fill out the spending worksheet, start with basic expenses: housing, food, taxes, health care, clothing, transportation, insurance, and—yes—savings, which you can't afford to stop contributing to, especially in your early retirement years. (Many experts recommend that you save at least 5 percent to 10 percent of your income *all* of your life.) Here are some tips that may help you arrive at your own estimated costs.

Housing

This expense won't change unless you pay off your mortgage, or sell your home and buy a smaller one in the same community, or move to a lower-cost town. The cost of homeowners' insurance, property taxes, upkeep, and utilities won't be much different after you retire.

Food

If you eat out less—for example, you won't have to buy lunch at work—this expense will decline, perhaps as much as 25 percent.

Taxes

Unless you work full-time or part-time in retirement, you will no longer have to pay Social Security and Medicare taxes on wages, which can reach as high as 7.65 percent. But, depending on your income, you may have to pay income tax on up to 85 percent of your Social Security income. On the other hand, some states will exempt all of that federal tax from their taxes.

Health Care

This expense is tough to calculate; you usually have no way of knowing whether you'll contract a chronic illness. The Urban Institute reports that a person aged 65 to 69 spends an average of $2,142 a year on medical bills; for people in their eighties, that amount jumps to $4,117 annually. Unless your employer provides supplemental medical insurance to retirees, you'll have to buy your own policy to cover costs not paid by Medicare. And don't overlook dental costs, which may not be covered by insurance.

Here's a guideline that might help you with your budgeting: Set aside a minimum of 1½ times the amount of your present health insurance policy's deductible, and earmark it for annual out-of-pocket medical expenses.

Clothing

You can expect real savings—30 percent or so—unless the job you left didn't require expensive suits or dresses. In retirement, every day is dress-down Friday.

Transportation

Wave goodbye to commuting costs. However, you may want to go on the long, expensive trips that you've been dreaming about for years but had to postpone because of job demands.

Recreation

This last category brings up the knotty subject of expenses that are called "FUN" in Worksheet 1. These aren't

necessary expenses. Many people spend perfectly happy re-
tirements at home, with perhaps an occasional trip to visit
their kids. Most, however, look forward to having the
leisure time to do what they want to do. But will you have
enough discretionary income? And if you're married, do
you and your spouse agree on how you'll spend your
leisure hours?

If you aren't in 100 percent agreement—and who is?—
you and your spouse should draw up separate lists of every
leisure activity you would like to pursue, from annual trips
abroad to frequent forays at a golf club. Quite possibly, you
won't have enough income in retirement to pay for both
your wish lists, so you'll have to adjust.

Now, here are some tips that will help you fill out the
savings worksheet on pages 319–320.

Social Security

You're probably familiar with the debate in Washington on
how to keep Social Security solvent. If you're in your mid-
fifties, don't worry about whether Congress will cause
your benefit to shrink. Politicians don't want to incur the
wrath of voters on the brink of retirement. So on line 2 of
Worksheet 2, insert the benefit that the Social Security Administration has estimated for you. (Call 1-800-772-1213 for
a copy.)

But if you're in your thirties or forties, how much you
can expect to receive may be uncertain. Ask the Social Security Administration for a benefit estimate every year so that
you won't be caught by surprise if your benefit shrinks or if
you must work longer for a full benefit.

Your Pension

We're referring here to a traditional, defined-benefit pension—one that doesn't require contributions from you. Ask your employer's benefits office to estimate your pension in today's dollars. (The worksheet will adjust the figure for future inflation.)

Your Current Savings and Investments

Include the balances of all your tax-deferred retirement accounts—IRAs, SEPs, Keoghs, 401(k)s, 403(b)s, and so on—as well as what you've tucked away in taxable savings and investments. If you're certain to receive a rich inheritance, add it to the total.

After you've totaled your expected spending and calculated your probable retirement income, you face the moment of reckoning. Is the number on the plus side? If it is, you're one of the lucky few. More likely, an ominous minus sign is attached to the figure. If so, take immediate action.

First, consider ways to cut your retirement costs. You might put off retiring for a few years, thus increasing your Social Security income and giving you more time to save. Or you can work part-time in retirement; landing a decent job is easier than ever. Or you might give up the dream of leaving your kids a substantial amount of money. Finally, consider reducing your retirement lifestyle or skipping the less important pastimes you're planning.

If any of these suggestions works for you, redo the worksheet. Quite possibly, there will still be a gap—but let's hope that it's a more manageable one.

Congratulations! You've begun a solid saving and investing program. But don't make the mistake of thinking that you can craft your plans and fill out the worksheets only once. As time passes, your interests and needs will change. To keep your savings on track, redo the worksheets each year, and change your savings accordingly. This step can help you achieve the kind of worry-free retirement that you deserve.

LET YOUR COMPUTER DO THE WORK

You can simplify your retirement chores immensely with either low-cost software or free resources available on the Internet.

First, here are three key questions and the outstanding websites that will help answer them for free:

1. How long can you expect to live? You need the answer to make sure you save enough money so that you won't ever go broke. Try Northwestern Mutual Life's longevity game (http://www .northwesternmutual.com).

2. How much money will you need for retirement? Call up Kiplinger's calculator (www.kiplinger.com /tools).

3. How fast are your savings growing? Also visit Kiplinger's compound-interest calculator (www .kiplinger.com/tools).

WORKSHEET 1

HOW MUCH YOU WILL SPEND IN RETIREMENT

Use this worksheet to estimate the cost of your retirement lifestyle. List both your current annual expenses and those you expect to incur in retirement. Use current dollars in this worksheet. Your annual savings goal, taking inflation into account, is stated on line 9 of Worksheet 2.

Annual Expense	**Today**	**In Retirement**
1. *Housing* (Include rent or mortgage payments, utilities, taxes, insurance, and other costs.)	_____	_____
2. *Food* (Include restaurant meals.)	_____	_____
3. *Taxes* (Don't include Social Security taxes after you retire from your present job unless you expect to work.)	_____	_____
4. *Healthcare* (Include insurance premiums and dentists' bills.)	_____	_____
5. *Clothing and Incidentals* (Include items such as cosmetics and visits to hairdressers and barbers.)	_____	_____
6. *Transportation* (Include auto and commuting expenses, but not vacation travel expenses.)	_____	_____

Calculate What You Will Need in Retirement

Annual Expense	Today	In Retirement
7. *Fun* (Include all recreation expenses: sports events, golf, stage show and movie tickets, books, CDs, video purchases and rentals, and cable-TV fees.)	_____	_____
8. *Travel* (Include holiday trips to visit parents or kids; seniors' trips— usually three to five day—as well as lengthier vacations in the United States or abroad.)	_____	_____
9. *Education* (Include your kids'costs, as well as your own.)	_____	_____
10. *Relatives* (Include financial support you give to those not living with you.)	_____	_____
11. *Loans* (Include credit-card payments.)	_____	_____
12. *Insurance* (Include all premiums except those for health and homeowners' policies, which are counted on lines 1 and 4.)	_____	_____
13. *Savings and Investments*	_____	_____

Annual Expense	Today	In Retirement
14. *Gifts* (Include charitable contributions.)	_____	_____
15. *Other* (Include everything you didn't include in lines 1 to 14.	_____	_____
16. *Total Annual Expenses* (add lines 1 through 15)	_____	_____
17. *Percentage of Current Income*	100%	_____*

*To safely estimate your living costs, the amount here should be close to 80 percent of today's *Total Annual Expenses*. If it's not, go back and adjust the Worksheet until you achieve 80 percent. This dollar amount—*Total Annual Expenses* in retirement—should be the one entered on line 1 of Worksheet 2.

W O R K S H E E T   2

How Much You Must Save Before Retiring

Use this worksheet, together with Worksheet 1, to calculate how much you must set aside each year. This worksheet is based on one prepared by Moss Adams, an accounting firm in Seattle. To be sure you err on the side of safety, the worksheet makes these assumptions: You will live to age 92; your investments will earn 8 percent a year; and inflation will run at 5 percent a year (the average for the past three decades).

1. *Annual Expenses in Retirement* (Use the figure from line 16 [*In Retirement* column], Worksheet 1 on pages 316–318 or, if you skipped the worksheet, 80 percent of your current income.) _____

2. *Estimated Annual Social Security Benefit* (If the Social Security Administration hasn't sent you an estimate, call 1-800-772-1213 and ask for one.) _____

3. *Estimated Annual Pension Benefits* (Ask your company's employee-benefits counselor for an estimate in today's dollars.) _____

4. *Annual Retirement Income Needed from Savings and Investments* (Subtract lines 2 and 3 from line 1.) _____

5. *How Much You Must Save by the Time You Retire* (Multiply line 4 above by Factor A below.) _____

6. *How Much You've Already Saved* (Include IRAs, 401(k)s, and other tax-deferred retirement plans, plus all other investments.) _____

7. *Inflation-Adjusted Value of Your Savings at Retirement* (Multiply line 6 above by Factor B below.) _____

8. *Total Retirement Capital You Still Need to Accumulate*
   (Subtract line 7 above from line 5 above.) _____

9. *How Much You Must Save Each Year Until Retirement*
   (Multiply line 8 above by Factor C below.) _____

Age at Retirement	55	56	57	58	59	60	61	62	63	64	65
Factor A	22.2	21.8	21.5	21.1	20.8	20.4	20.0	19.6	19.2	18.8	18.3

Years to Retirement	3	9	15	20	25	30
Factor B	1.09	1.30	1.56	1.81	2.09	2.43
Factor C	0.324	0.098	0.054	0.037	0.027	0.021

Get Some Free Help
from Uncle Sam

Worried about retirement? About how much money you'll need to get by comfortably, or whether you have accumulated enough already? You'd be surprised at how much solid guidance, on these and other subjects, is available now—free—from the U.S. Government. This week, call, write away, or go online, for some gratis information and advice.

Here, with full credit to the American Savings Education Council in Washington, DC (www.asec.org), is a guide to some of the resources that are yours for the asking, and how to get them.

- The Social Security Administration (SSA), in response to your request, will send you a Social Security Statement that shows the benefits you and your family will be eligible for if you retire, become disabled, or die. When you get the statement, check it carefully and report any missing or changed data. To request your statement, call the SSA at 1-800-772-1213, or visit its website at www.ssa.gov.

- The Department of Labor's Pension and Welfare Benefits Administration (PWBA) can help you learn about saving for retirement. Ask for its brochure: "Top Ten Ways to Beat the Clock and Prepare for Retirement." The PWBA also publishes "What You Should Know About Your Pension Rights" and "Protect Your Pension." Get them by calling 1-800-998-7542 or by visiting www.dol.gov/dol/pwba.

- The Department of Agriculture offers various educational programs in personal finance, with an emphasis on retirement. These are provided by the department's Cooperative State Research, Education and Extension Service, through its partner universities and county offices nationwide. To find out what's available near you, contact your local Cooperative Extension Service (often located in a courthouse, a post office, or other government building). The website is www.reeusda.gov/statepartners/usa.htm.

- The Internal Revenue Service has many guides to help you understand some of the key financial issues you will face in retirement. To find out what the IRS offers, see Publication 910, *Guide to Free Tax Services*. To order IRS publications, phone 1–800-TAX-FORM (1-800-329-3676). You can access the IRS website at www.irs.gov, and download publications or request help via E-mail.

- For a copy of two helpful brochures—the "Treasury Direct Investor's Kit," and "U.S. Savings Bonds Investor

Information"—write to the Bureau of the Public Debt, Parkersburg, WV 26106-1328. To learn the current interest rate for U.S. Savings Bonds, call 1-800-4USBOND (1-800-487-2663). You can also visit the Bureau's websites at www.publicdebt.treas.gov or www.savingsbonds.gov.

- The Federal Trade Commission (FTC) gives this advice: "Invest in opportunities you know something about. Be skeptical of strangers selling investments over the phone. Try to get a second opinion from a financial planner, accountant or attorney." The FTC has several publications on how to recognize and avoid bogus investment schemes. Write or call the Consumer Response Center, Federal Trade Commission, CRC-240, Washington, DC; phone 1-877-FTC-HELP, or visit the FTC's website at www.ftc.gov.

- The American Savings Education Council (ASEC), a coalition of private and government institutions, has a host of publications, including a useful worksheet titled "Ballpark Estimate." Request it and fill it out. It will give you a basic idea of the savings that you'll need when you retire. You can write to the ASEC, 2121 K Street, NW, Suite 600, Washington, DC 20037–1896; phone: 1-202-775-9130 or 1-202-659-0670.

- The Federal Consumer Information Center, in Pueblo, Colorado deserves special mention. It publishes more than 200 useful booklets, and distributes millions of them either free or for a modest charge (50 cents is typical). To order, visit the Center online at www.pueblo.gsn.gov, or phone 1-888-878-3256 (that's 1-888-8PUEBLO).

Here is a sampling of the Center's titles: *Buying a New Car; Nine Ways to Lower Your Auto Insurance Costs; Danger in Your Home (and How to Make It a Safer Place); Learning Disabilities; Parents' Guide to the Internet; All About Direct Loans (for College); Are There Any Public Lands for Sale?; Medicare & You 2000; How to Buy a Home With a Low Down Payment; Looking for the Best Mortgage—Shop, Compare, Negotiate; Home Electrical Safety Check; Establishing a Trust Fund; Making a Will; Planning Your Estate; What You Should Know About Buying Life Insurance; Understanding Opportunities & Risks in Futures Trading; All That Glitters: The Jive on Jewelry; Shop Safely Online; Where to Write for Vital Records (Birth, Marriage, Divorce, and Death Certificates).*

Finally, here's a short list of useful phone numbers. To find out more about:

- The phone number for just about any federal government agency, call 1-800-688-9889.
- Automobile safety recalls, call 1-800-424-9393, or, within Washington, DC, 1-202-366-0123.
- Other product recalls: 1-800-638-2772.
- Education grants and loans: 1-800-433-3243.
- Veterans' benefits: 1-800-827-1000.

Beware the Lure of Tax-Deferred Annuities

How would you react if a trusted broker, banker, insurance agent, financial planner, or other financial adviser offered you an investment with these seductive features: (1) tax-deferral on your earnings until you withdraw them, (2) no limit on your contributions, and (3) guaranteed lifetime income in retirement for you *and* your spouse?

You'd be wise to react cautiously. The salesperson is trying to interest you in an annuity, and it may indeed give you the benefits that he or she promises. But most people can get all of those benefits and more, at far less cost, with other investments. Though they have become highly popular, annuities suit only a small minority of investors, and even they must shop with extreme care to avoid overpaying or locking themselves into a low-return turkey.

This week, spend some time studying annuities and determining what role, if any, they should play in your financial plan.

Basically, an annuity is a mutual-fund-like portfolio of investments, sponsored by an insurance company or a bank, that provides both future income and insurance. It promises to pay you regular sums—on a fixed or variable basis—for a specified time—usually, from the day you retire to the end of your life, and perhaps the end of your spouse's life, too. The insurance part of the contract ensures that your heirs will get back at least the money you invest in the annuity. Because annuities are insurance products, taxes on their earnings are deferred; you don't pay taxes on them until you start taking them out as income. Consequently, they can grow at an extra-fast rate.

Contracts called *single-premium* annuities generally require initial investments of $5,000 to $10,000 or more. Other contracts, called *flexible-premium* annuities, allow you to start by putting in as little as $25 a month, or even less. Unlike Individual Retirement Accounts (IRAs), you contribute as much as you want each year. And unlike many IRAs, your contributions to annuities must come from after-tax income.

The trouble is, annuities are heavily laden with fees. There are usually no front-end loads. Instead, a one-time sales commission, ranging from 3 percent to 8 percent of your investment, is taken out of your account's earnings. And the insurance company or other sponsors deduct roughly 2 percent a year from your account, for insurance and management costs.

Most companies also sock you with big surrender fees if you make substantial withdrawals in the earlier years of the contract. These fees can run as high as 15 percent of your total account balance if you pull money out in the first year of the contract. After that, the fee typically declines about one percentage point a year until it disappears in seven to 15 years.

There is one escape hatch: Many insurers let you withdraw 10 percent annually from your account without surrender charges. But if you are under age 59½, the IRS will hit you with a 10 percent penalty plus regular income taxes on the earnings included in the withdrawal.

Because of these fees, you should not consider buying an annuity unless you meet the following conditions:

- You are regularly contributing the maximum to all tax-deferred retirement accounts available to you, including 401(k)s, 403(b)s, IRAs, Simplified Employee Pensions (SEPs), and Keogh plans. All provide the same tax advantages as annuities—but at lower cost.
- You are in at least the 28 percent tax bracket now, and you feel confident that your bracket will be lower after retirement. If that description doesn't apply, an annuity's fees may wipe out its tax advantages.
- You have carefully considered investing in tax-free municipal bonds and have concluded that you would do better with an annuity, even after paying taxes on the earnings at withdrawal. Lately, high-rated (AAA) 30-year munis have been yielding a tax-free 5.5 percent, equivalent to 7.64 percent for investors in the 28 percent bracket, and 9.11 percent for those in the top 39.6 percent bracket.
- You are willing to tie up your money in an investment for as long as 15 years, or as many years as it will take the surrender charge to decline to zero. If your annuity's investments start lagging, you'll have

to hang on until the fee has dropped to a point where transferring your money to another annuity makes sense. (Remember: If you withdraw your money before you turn 59½, you'll have to pay a 10 percent tax penalty.)

Essentially, there are two kinds of annuities, and they suit entirely different types of people:

1. *Immediate annuities* are popular with retirees because the contracts start paying regular (usually monthly) income right away. You typically buy them with a lump sum, perhaps from a retirement account, and they guarantee to pay you income for the rest of your life, and, if you wish, the rest of your spouse's life. A major shortcoming is: Your income stays the same over the years, even though your cost of living will inevitably rise.

2. *Deferred annuities* appeal mostly to middle-aged investors who are piling up money for retirement and want to defer taxes on their investment earnings. You buy them either with a lump sum or with installment payments. You usually don't start receiving income until after you turn 59½ (because of the tax penalty) and are retired. Then, you can take your money as a lump sum, or make periodic withdrawals, or annuitize it. (The withdrawal options are explained later.)

You must make one further choice. Depending on how you want your money invested, you must designate a fixed-rate or a variable-rate annuity.

1. *Fixed-rate annuities* appeal to very conservative investors. The sponsoring insurance company guarantees a specific interest rate, usually for a year but sometimes up to 10 years. Lately, fixed-rate annuities have paid 5.5 percent to 6.85 percent a year. When the guarantee period ends, the company announces its return for the next year. Rates depend on the performance of the insurer's investments—typically, Treasury and corporate bonds, and home mortgages. The insurance company usually guarantees a minimal 3 percent annual return.

2. *Variable-rate annuities* attract investors who want higher returns than are available with fixed-rate annuities, and are willing to tolerate payouts that fluctuate. The insurer offers you an assortment of funds, called subaccounts, that invest in the stock, bond, and money markets and are managed by well-known mutual fund companies such as Dreyfus, Fidelity, and Neuberger & Berman. Typically, you can choose among seven subaccounts, or sometimes as many as 30. Each has different investment objectives.

Within the stock category, subaccounts may include aggressive growth, blue-chip, and international equities. Bond subaccounts include corporate, Treasury, and high-yield issues. Most insurers also offer a money market subaccount.

You allocate your money as you wish, and, by phone, you can switch among subaccounts with no charge. Your annual returns—and your eventual payout—depend on your skill in choosing investments. Best advice: Put your money in stock and bond funds with strong growth records. Otherwise, your yields won't be rich enough to make up for the annuity's fees.

If you think an annuity is the right investment for you, take these steps before you buy.

1. *Deal only with the most reliable insurers.* Look for those with top financial ratings: at least A+ from A.M. Best, Aa– from Moody's Investors Service, or AA– from Standard & Poor's. Your annuity salesperson can provide these ratings, or you can consult the rating firms' publications at a large public library.

2. *Make sure the sponsor's annuities are top performers.* If you're shopping for a fixed-rate annuity, don't necessarily buy the one that promises the highest yield. Typically, it has a teaser rate and will fall three or more percentage points in subsequent years. Ask to see the rates the sponsor has paid over the past 10 years.

You can compare the rates of the 100 biggest fixed annuities by consulting a newsletter: *Comparative Annuity Reports.* If you can't find a copy in your library, order one from the newsletter at P.O. Box 1268, Fair Oaks, CA 95628, or phone 1-916-487-7863. The cost is $10 a month or $80 a year.

Make sure that the insurance company's interest rate floor—the minimum you'll receive—exceeds 4.5 percent. With a variable-rate annuity, research the subaccounts' performance over the past three years and compare it with their investment category averages. You can find these figures through Morningstar's *Variable Annuity/Life Performance Report* (www.morningstar.com) or WebAnnuities.com (1-800-872-6684 or www.webannuities.com), which provides free quotes and publishes the semi-annual *Annuity Shopper* (single issue: $25; one-year subscription: $45). You can get copies from your salesperson or find them at large public libraries.

Compare the performance figures *after* expenses have been deducted. If the subaccounts that interest you don't have three-year records—or if the salesperson balks at helping you find comparative data—shop elsewhere.

3. *Favor low-expense annuities.* You usually should avoid annuities with total annual expenses that exceed about 2 percent a year. Still, you might consider a high-fee annuity if its subaccounts have strong performance records that make up for the excessive fees. Your salesperson can show you a breakdown of the annuity's fees.

To get the lowest fee, you might consider buying a low-load contract directly from the sponsor. You can get a list of discount brokerages and mutual fund companies that sell these annuities in your area by calling the local offices of large mutual-fund sponsors, such as Dreyfus, Fidelity, and Vanguard.

4. *Insist on a bailout clause with a fixed-rate annuity.* This essential provision enables you to withdraw your money if you think the renewal rate is too low. Most companies offer an option that lets you do so without penalty, provided the new rate is, say, one or two percentage points lower than the previous one. If you bail out, you can transfer the money to another company's annuity and avoid paying taxes. Be sure to fill out the Internal Revenue Service's Form 1035 (an exchange form), which you can get from the new company.

When you retire, you can take all your money out of the annuity, but you'll have to pay income taxes on the earnings. To postpone the taxes, you can set up a systematic withdrawal plan, telling the insurance company how much cash to send you from your account each month. Each amount will include some principal and some taxable earnings. You can raise, lower, or stop the payments as you wish.

This approach still has a major shortcoming: Your annuity could run out of money in your lifetime. To prevent this, you can annuitize, which simply means you turn over the value of your annuity to an insurer, in return for a guaranteed monthly income. (Each payment will include both taxable earnings and nontaxable return of principal.) You'll have four basic choices:

1. *Life annuity.* You get the biggest checks with this choice, and they will continue for your lifetime—but *only your* lifetime. This is an excellent choice for a single person or someone whose spouse will have sufficient income from other sources. There's one drawback: If you die before the insurer thinks you will, you won't get all the income you were entitled to receive with life-with-certain-period plan.

2. *Joint-and-survivor annuity.* By accepting roughly 7 percent less income than with a life plan, you can take an annuity that, if you die first, will continue making payments to your spouse or another dependent for as long as he or she lives. This is the best payout choice for most couples. Depending on your preference, your spouse can receive 50 percent of your payout after you die or, if you're willing to accept slightly less income during your lifetime, 100 percent of it.

3. *Life-with-certain-period annuity.* With this option, you get a lifetime income plus a guarantee of payments for 10 years or so. If you die within that time, your beneficiary collects the remaining payments. This is an excellent alternative for someone who would otherwise take a life annuity but has reason to believe that he or she will die prematurely, perhaps from some long-term illness.

4. *Term-certain annuity.* You and your surviving spouse get annuity payments for a fixed number of years. If you both die before the term ends, the remaining payments go to your heirs. But if one (or both) of you outlives the term, you won't collect any more payments.

To repeat: Before buying an annuity, be absolutely sure that you can't do better with another investment. If you have maxed out on your tax-deferred retirement accounts, you may still get a higher return elsewhere—at least over a period of 15 years or so—because of annuities' high fees.

Guard Against Fraud

They're *b-a-a-a-ck*. The scam artists are out again in force—those unscrupulous con men (and women), crooks, and assorted lowlifes who are trying all sorts of phony stock deals, common frauds, and other tricks to separate you from your hard-earned money. Spend part of this week educating yourself and your family about the dangers of consumer fraud.

Watch out for hard-selling types who cold-call you at home or knock on your door during dinner to try to whet your appetite for raw investments. Beware also of those who dangle fly-by-night schemes that they vow can't miss. If an unknown salesperson phones and pitches a stock to you, you're smart to hang up. You've got better things to chew on. At a minimum, ask him or her to call back tomorrow and outline his or her plan to your banker or financial planner. (You'll probably never get the second call.)

Be particularly cautious of someone who refuses to provide references from present customers or a warranty for a *real* product (not just a dream) that he or she is selling. Be suspicious of any seller who says you have to make up your mind and send in your money very fast. Ask for at least 48 hours to contemplate the purchase or investment.

You probably think you'd never fall for this one: A smooth-talking salesperson urges you, over the phone, to grab a once-in-a-lifetime chance to invest $10,000 in a gold mine, and promises to let you buy the gold at two-thirds the market price. You're too smart to be taken in by that obviously phony pitch, right? Well, don't be too sure. Scamsters rob Americans of over $40 billion a year, says the Alliance Against Fraud in Telemarketing and Electronic Commerce. *Money* magazine has estimated that stock fraud alone costs investors as much as $10 billion a year.

The victims aren't all ignorant suckers. A study for the American Association of Retired Persons (AARP) found that people who lose money in scams—from hollow investments to phony job opportunities, fake prizes, and home-repair cons—tend to be more affluent and better educated than the average citizen.

Anybody can be an innocent victim, but scamsters particularly love to prey on the elderly. People over 65 make up 12.7 percent of the U.S. population and 30 percent of the victims of telemarketing fraud. Maybe that's because, as the AARP study says, older people are quicker to believe promises and slower to take steps to protect their legal rights than the population as a whole.

You could indeed be targeted by a con artist—usually by phone, but sometimes by mail or by messages sent to computer chat rooms and E-mail addresses. Unless you know how to detect and deal with an incoming flim-flam, you could easily become a victim.

Make no mistake: Many con artists are masters at making their phony investments—or supposedly infallible stock-picking skills—sound real. For example, a broker might try to persuade you to invest $1,000 or so in penny stocks—shares of a firm with an obscure name, that are trading for less than a dollar each—so that he or she can prove to you that his or her recommendations will make money for you. Sure enough, the stock soars in a few weeks. The broker then calls back and urges you to put, say, $10,000 in a second stock. You bite, and the stock plunges. Why? Because the broker has dumped his or her shares and driven the price down, just as he or she pushed the first stock's price up by heavy buying. Typically, the trouble is that you invested ten times as much money in the losing stock as in the winner.

Or consider this often-successful ploy: A polite, well-spoken caller introduces himself as "Mr. Martingale" and tells you that he doesn't want your money—only a chance to prove his stock-picking talents. As evidence, he assures you that, according to his research, the stock of XYZ Corp. will rise by the end of the week. Sure enough, by Friday, the price is up. He calls early the following week and forecasts that UVW Co.'s stock will fall by Friday. Again, he's right. After a couple more weeks of accurate predictions, could you become so confident of his skills that you would be willing to have him invest your money? If so, say goodbye to your hard-won cash, for you would have fallen for the aptly named "infallible-investor scam."

What you don't know is that the forecaster has made hundreds of calls, telling half the people that XYZ stock will go up and the other half that it will go down. His second calls go only to the people who got the correct prediction. He keeps doing this for a couple more weeks. By then, only a fraction of his targets are left. But if 30 investors give him $15,000 each, the con artist can disappear with $450,000. Not bad pay for a month's work.

Other popular scams offer unwary investors: shares in partnerships that operate 900 telephone numbers (the ones that typically charge $5 a minute or $25 a call); federal licenses to operate paging services, mobile radio systems, and wireless cable-TV shows; phony medical devices to treat arthritis and other painful illnesses; and, most brazen of all, offers to recoup the victim's losses from past scams—for a fat fee.

If somebody calls you, unsolicited, and tries to sell you something over the phone, you're probably wise to get rid of him or her—fast. Be particularly suspicious of phone callers who breathlessly announce that you have won a prize, but also declare that you must immediately send in some money—and your credit-card number—to claim the prize. *Always* ask for the caller's phone number and address. Beware of anyone who has only an anonymous P.O. box or refuses to give you a phone number for a return call at another time.

Scamsters typically select potential victims from real estate tax rolls, magazine subscription lists, and sucker (or "mooch") lists that they buy from each other. As a result, if you're tricked once—even for as little as a $10 jar of cosmetics—you're likely to be called again.

Most scamsters operate out of cramped offices—called "boiler rooms"—in California, Florida, Nevada, and Texas. Salespeople may reach you on specially rigged phones that filter out the background din to give you the impression that the caller is in a quiet office suite. The pitch, read from a prepared script, is always smooth and grabby. Often, the salesperson will claim that you'll be able to deduct the entire investment from your income taxes—which is true, but you'll be deducting it as a capital LOSS.

Here, according to business writer Frank Merrick, are eleven signs that a person you are talking to on the phone may be a scamster. Hang up immediately if you recognize any of the following:

1. A caller guarantees you a high return with little risk. After several years in which even blue-chip stocks returned 25 percent or more a year, this may sound plausible. Nonetheless, investments with high potential returns are always risky.
2. A caller assures you of a specific return. No matter how modest it may be, don't bite. No one can guarantee a return on anything except a bank savings account—and that's not really an investment.
3. A caller tells you about an investment that has been approved by the Internal Revenue Service. The IRS doesn't endorse investments.
4. A caller offers you a chance to get into a business that has been in the headlines recently—for example, an Internet or genetics-research stock. Scamsters

often make their sham investments sound up-to-date.

5. A caller assures you that an investment is as safe as a bank certificate of deposit. Unless you believe in Santa Claus, don't believe that pitch.

6. A caller implies that a firm—which you've never heard of—is associated with a well-known Wall Street powerhouse. Actually, the big-name firm simply executes the small firm's trades.

7. A caller claims to have connections that will get you a special deal on a stock—say, at a below-market price—or inside information that a stock will soon soar.

8. A caller demands an immediate decision and warns that you'll be sorry if you miss this opportunity. Don't listen. A sound investment will still be around tomorrow, or even next week.

9. A caller gives you the runaround when you ask for written verification of his or her credentials or of an offer. For instance, you might be told: "The opportunity will expire before the documents could reach you." Trust me, if it's a legitimate deal, it won't.

10. A caller says he or she wants to help you make money, "Just as I've been doing for my friends, relatives, business colleagues [some names might even be real ones] and for members of your church [or college alumni association, or a social organization]." This is the well-known "affinity fraud."

Somehow, the con man has obtained a membership list or has persuaded a previous phone contact sucker to name his friends, relatives, and associates.

11. A caller offers to have your check picked up by a private overnight-express service, or asks you to the send the check via that kind of service. This may indicate that the caller wants to avoid mail-fraud charges.

Here are four steps you can take to protect yourself:

1. Ask for the caller's CRD number. The Central Registration Depository, maintained by the North American Securities Administrators Association (NASAA) and the National Association of Securities Dealers (NASD), keeps track of all registered brokers and their disciplinary history.

2. Call the NASD (1-800-289-9999) or your state securities agency to check out the caller's background. You can get the state office's phone number from the NASD or by calling the NASAA at 1-888-846-2722. If the state agency doesn't have a record of the caller's name and CRD number, he or she isn't registered in your state and, legally, shouldn't be trying to sell you an investment. If the broker is hawking commodities, check out his name and credentials with the Disciplinary Information Access Line, run by the National Futures Association (1-800-676-4632).

3. Ask for a prospectus or other printed documents describing the investment, as well as a brochure

describing the caller's firm. Federal law requires that you be given them on request. But don't fully trust what the caller sends you. Scamsters have been known to send phony performance records to victims, so be sure to take the next step.

4. Check out the investment opportunity independently. If it's a stock, look it up in the *Value Line Investment Survey* and the Standard & Poor's stock reports. Both are available at large libraries. You can ask the company's investor relations office for free copies of the firm's annual report and the company's annual 10K and quarterly 10Q statements, which are filed with the Securities and Exchange Commission. You can also get them from the SEC for a copying fee (call 202-942-8090), or get them free at the SEC's website (http://www.sec.gov/edaux/searches.htm). Then talk over the investment with other advisers, such as your broker, your financial planner, and/or your accountant.

If you've been conned by a scamster, you can file complaints with the following sources of free information and assistance:

1. Your state attorney general; you'll find the address and telephone number in your phone book.
2. The Federal Trade Commission, Telemarketing Fraud, Room 200, 6th Street and Pennsylvania Avenue NW, Washington, DC 20580. For a booklet that lists your rights, call the FTC at 1-202-326-2222.
3. The National Fraud Information Center, a private nonprofit organization: 1-800-876-7060.

4. The Alliance Against Fraud in Telemarketing (1-202-835-3323), which offers a free brochure, *Schemes, Scams and Flim-Flams,* that provides advice on how to avoid being taken by con artists.
5. Call for Action, a Washington, DC-based network of radio and TV consumer hotlines; 1-202-537-0585.

WEEK

50

Find Your Best Deals in Checking Accounts

All checking accounts used to be very much alike, but now that's radically changed. In their fierce competition to win your business, banks are making all sorts of special offers. Be smart: Shop around, among several banks, to see which one offers your best deals in checking.

Here are some tips:

- Try to keep all your checking, savings, CDs, and other business in the same bank. If the money in those combined accounts adds up to a certain total, you should get free checking and a number of other deals—like a free safe-deposit box.
- If you write very few checks, use a bank money market account *instead of* a checking account. These accounts place limits on the frequency of check writing or withdrawals, and often require a minimum balance. But you may collect more interest than the

puny one-half percent or one percent that a checking account may pay.

- Look for a bank that charges you nothing for withdrawing cash from its ATM machines. Ideally, you want a bank that gives you free withdrawals not only from its own ATMs, but also from the machines of some other banks.
- Look for a bank that offers you online access to your checking account, allowing you to monitor your balance, transfer money between your accounts, and do almost all your other banking electronically.
- Look for a bank that will automatically—and for free!—pay some of your bills for you, such as your mortgage or your car loan. All you have to do is give instructions electronically or by phone. Even if your bank doesn't offer online bill paying, many other institutions do—read Week 9, "Master the Computer" for more details.

The right checking account for you depends on more than the size of your balance. Banks are eager to personalize their dealings with customers, so students, retirees, and members of the military should look for checking accounts that target *their* needs. For example:

- Students and minors may be entitled to a number of extras—a lower minimum opening deposit, no minimum balance on a checking account, no-annual-fee credit cards, and free unlimited use of the bank's ATMs.
- Men and women in the armed services may be exempt from monthly maintenance fees if they keep a

certain dollar amount in a related Military Savings Account.

- Retirees may get extras ranging from free travelers checks to postage-paid bank-by-mail, a worthwhile service for elders who are unable to travel to the bank.

One example of an institution that has many special offers is the First Citizens Bank, with branches in North Carolina, Virginia, and West Virginia. If you keep $3,500 in a regular savings account or $5,000 in a bank money market account—and as much or as little as you like in a checking account—you can get special rates on CDs and consumer loans, a no-annual-fee credit card, and a free VISA Check-Card, which doubles as an ATM card.

You may want to consider opening a checking account in another state, which can be particularly convenient if you travel often to a specific destination. Interest rates vary by state, and local banks that are hungry for your business may offer relatively high rates and special checking deals.

You should let your bank work for you, not only by providing a checking account that is right for your balance and expenditures, but also one that helps you keep excellent records of all your transactions.

Many banks will simply send out a photocopy of your canceled checks, but you often can get the original check back for your records by calling your bank to request it. You don't have to wait for the mail if you use online checking; a scan of your canceled checks should appear on your screen immediately. Also, if your bank charges you to see your last few transactions on the ATM machine's screen, you may want to think about switching banks—or at least using a free online checking service to review your account. Some banks let you access their websites to see a sample of what your electronic checking records will look like if you go online. Look for user-friendly programs that are clear and organized.

The bottom line: Before you write your next check, *check* out all of your options.

Get on Headhunters' Lists

So many people are hopping from job to job that the U.S. labor market is beginning to look like a French bedroom farce. Or one big temp agency.

There's a lusty demand for smart, skilled people, and the headhunters have never been busier. Says Peter Felix, president of the Association of Executive Search Consultants: "Right now there's a great shortage of really outstanding people as we change from the old economy to the new economy. There will continue to be a demographic shortage of men and women of the right age with the right talents."

Headhunter Linda Bialecki, who has her own firm in New York City, agrees: "The number of 33- to 44-year-olds will be decreasing over the next 15 years. That's one reason why compensation is going through the roof."

So, if you want a better job, you've never had a better chance. What you need to do, particularly if you're a manager or a techie, is to get noticed by headhunters—get on the A lists of searchers who troll for talent.

To accomplish that, take charge of your career and don't fall in love with any job.

As a first step, brush up your resume and send it to the headhunters, particularly the Big Four: (1) Heidrick and Struggles; (2) Korn Ferry; (3) Spencer Stuart; and (4) Russell Reynolds. That ploy wouldn't have worked a few years ago, but now recruiters are so eager, or so desperate, to find talent that they're casting a wider net—and paying attention to resumes. (Whenever you get a promotion or a new job, visit them at www.heidrick.com, www.kornferry.com, www.spencerstuart.com, and www.russellreynolds.com and learn how to register your resume with them online.)

Do all you can to make yourself stand out from the crowd. Says recruiter Hob Brown of Russell Reynolds: "Be very aware of how you present yourself to the analysts, accountants, lawyers, and I-bankers you deal with, because headhunters will call those people for references."

Become active in professional groups, and attend industry conferences. The headhunters often go to them, hungrily looking for stars. You can approach a recruiter, introduce yourself, and volunteer to help if the recruiter has a search going in your field. And if you're ever asked to give a public speech or write an article or get a profile of yourself on your employer's website, seize the opportunity—in fact, volunteer for it!

Try to get into a position where you *run something,* no matter how small. That's the surest way to show demonstrable *results* and get recognized. "We want to see increased revenue or a new product that you developed," says Brown.

You're better off in a troubled operation than a successful one because if you turn the failing operation around, you become a hero.

But don't become infatuated with any job and get stuck spending too much time in it, the headhunters advise. Jack Clarey of Chicago's Clarey and Andrews says the ideal is three years in a managerial position: "In the first year, you learn what you inherited. In the second year, you develop and execute your strategy. In the third year, we'll see if you're a genius or a dud."

And remember: When they're collecting evaluations of you, headhunters often consult with former employees of your company. So be *nice* to everybody.

What should you do if a headhunter calls you?

Be sure to *take* the call. Never brush off a headhunter or play too hard to get. Even if you're happy and secure in your job, you'd be wise to volunteer to help identify people in any of the recruiter's future searches. You might say something like, "I certainly won't leave my job now, but if I can help you, I'm pleased to do it." That is an invitation for the searcher to call again, and it keeps your lines open. You never know.

Summing Up

The more I see of the New Economy, the more I treasure the Old Verities.

These are the time-tested principles and practices that have enabled investors to survive and succeed in times of boom and bust alike. You have read about many of them in this book, and it doesn't hurt to repeat some of them now:

- Don't try to get rich quick. There is no way to do that, and making the attempt may cause you to risk too much, too often. Aim instead to become merely more affluent, and move toward that goal steadily, even slowly.

- Don't become too greedy. Don't believe that the trees grow to the skies. Nobody—but nobody—can consistently get in at the very bottom and get out at the very top.

- Do be prudent. If you have an investment that has surged in value, you might be wise to take some money off the table. Don't necessarily sell all the investment, but sell some of it—just in case.

- Don't panic when markets decline, as they inevitably will from time to time. Use the drop, perhaps, to scoop up some bargains.

- Have a bias for action. Favor stocks over bonds. Favor growth stocks over more conservative shares (particularly if you are young). Favor no-load mutual funds over load mutual funds. Favor discount brokers over full-service brokers (unless you need ongoing investment advice).

- Invest for the long term. For all their virtues, stocks can kill you in the short term.

- Invest on the installment plan, also known as dollar-cost-averaging. Put in the same, fixed amount of money every month or from every paycheck—whatever you can afford. When your investments go up, you can congratulate yourself for having earned some paper profits. When markets tank, you can figure that you are at a bargain sale. Last month your regular monthly installment of capital could buy, say, only three shares of your favorite mutual fund, but this month it can buy four shares.

- Allocate your assets. The greatest determinant of your success as an investor will not be your sagacity in selecting specific stocks, bonds or funds but the way you slice up your total portfolio into broad categories of, say, large-cap growth stocks and AAA bonds and so on.

History's lesson is that people who invested steadily and sensibly over the years have done very well. They wisely created an asset allocation formula, and they stuck with it, save for periodic strategic adjustments. They practiced dollar-cost-averaging. They diversified their investments. They invested for the long haul.

In closing, let me reiterate several lines:

—To thine own self be true. If you are a cautious, conservative person, you are probably well advised to follow a cautious, conservative money management style. Conversely, if you are optimistic and confident, you are probably wise to aim for capital growth.

—Nobody can put a price on your ability to sleep soundly at night.

—Bulls make money and bears make money, but *hogs* never make money.

Good Luck and Good Fortune!

INDEX

ABOUT THE AUTHOR

Marshall Loeb is a personal finance pioneer and has been managing editor of two of the most successful magazines in history, *Money* and *Fortune,* as well as business editor of *Time.* Most recently, he was editor of the *Columbia Journalism Review.* He is now a columnist for CBS Marketwatch.com, and a commentator on CBS Radio and the television show *Market Watch Weekend,* currently seen throughout the United States. Loeb has won nearly every major award in economic and financial journalism, and recently was named by a jury of his peers as one of the 100 most important business journalists of the twentieth century.